AMAZING ARCHAEOLOGISTS
AND THEIR FINDS

AMAZING ARCHAEOLOGISTS AND THEIR FINDS

William Scheller

The Oliver Press, Inc.
Minneapolis

J

J
920
ARCHAEOLOGISTS

Library of Congress Cataloging-in-Publication Data

Scheller, William
Amazing archaeologists and their finds / William Scheller.

p. cm.
Includes bibliographical references and index.
Contents: Austen Henry Layard, Hormuzd Rassam, and the lost
cities of Assyria—Henri Mouhot and Angkor—Heinrich
Schliemann and Troy—Sir Arthur Evans and Knossos—Edward
Thompson and the Sacred Well of Chichen Itza—Hiram Bingham
and Machu Picchu—Howard Carter and the Tomb of
Tutankhamen—Kathleen Kenyon and the biblical city of Jericho.
ISBN: 1-881508-17-X : $14.95
1. Archaeologists—Biography—Juvenile literature.
2. Archaeology—History—Juvenile literature. [1. Archaeologists.
2. Archaeology.] I. Title.
CC110.S34 1994
930.1'0902'2—dc20   93-46919
[B]   CIP
                                             AC

ISBN 1-8810508-17-X
Profiles XII
Printed in the United States of America

99 98 97 96 95 94   8 7 6 5 4 3 2 1

Contents

Archaeologists Howard Carter (left) and Arthur Callender wrap one of the two life-sized "guards" found at the tomb of Tutankhamen (now often called "King Tut") for shipment to the Egyptian Museum in Cairo.

Introduction

*D*eep inside an ancient Egyptian tomb, a man peers through a narrow gap in a wall into a room filled with golden treasures.

Digging in a desert oasis near Israel's Dead Sea, a woman uncovers the remains of what may be the oldest town on earth.

Inspired by a story he had read as a child, a man discovers the ruins of Troy—a city that many scholars believed had never existed.

Each of these trained and dedicated people working at these far-flung places is an archaeologist—a special kind of explorer who searches for the past of humankind. Since the beginning of human history, people have left objects that reveal the ways they worked and played, set up their households, worshiped their gods, fought their

Archaeologists believe that this statue, which ancient Egyptians placed in Tutankhamen's tomb more than 3,000 years ago, may have been designed in the king's image.

enemies, and buried their dead. These objects, called *artifacts*, spell out stories about the past. Artifacts are often all that can be "read" about bygone ages, since long-dead peoples may have left no written records of their lives and accomplishments, or they may have written in languages that people no longer use or understand.

An artifact can be just about anything made by human hands. It might be something as small as a broken piece of kitchen pottery or a bone needle for sewing animal skins. Or it could be enormous, like the great ruined buildings that have survived from the days of ancient

Greece. It might be buried underground like the ancient town of Jericho, or it might be standing for all to see, like the pyramids of Egypt. An artifact, whatever its size or location, is a piece of the vast and complex puzzle of human history.

Many people mistake archaeologists for paleontologists, and the differences between the two can be confusing. A paleontologist studies the development of humans and animals by looking at bones and fossils. This type of scientist examines the skeletons of prehistoric humans or tries to find out, for example, how dinosaurs lived by piecing together their fossilized bones.

While archaeologists, on the other hand, may discover human bones in an old tomb or at the scene of some ancient disaster, they are mostly interested in the objects that people made long ago and what those things say about how they lived.

Archaeologists must study history, of course—not only the history of human events but also the histories of art, language, religion, and even the earth's changing surface and climate. Understanding the materials from which things are made is also helpful. For instance, archaeologists can sometimes tell where a piece of pottery is from by identifying the minerals used in its shiny glaze.

If someone asked you to picture an archaeologist, chances are that you would probably imagine a person wearing rugged outdoor clothes and holding a shovel.

A modern sign marks the entrance to King Tut's tomb, one of the most famous archaeological sites in Egypt.

Archaeologists often work outside—sometimes in harsh climates. The reason so many artifacts of the past are buried beneath the surface of the earth is because of the earth itself and the ways in which people build their towns and cities. The earth's surface is always changing—sometimes very slowly over thousands of years and sometimes with sudden violence. Over the centuries, what was once a cave dwelling may fill up with mud and rock. What was once a village near a river may gradually be covered over with silt carried by the river's current. Likewise, the shifting sands of a desert can hide the ruins of an entire city.

Other changes can occur in a matter of minutes. When Mount Vesuvius erupted in A.D. 79, it buried the Roman city of Pompeii in a deep layer of ash. When an earthquake struck Jamaica in 1692, the capital city of Port Royal quickly sank beneath the waters of its harbor.

People also have a way of burying the things they make by "recycling" the very sites on which they built their homes. If a city had a good location—if it was built along a fine harbor or on a river useful for travel and shipping—its inhabitants might replace old buildings with new ones on the same spots, even on the same foundations. This practice created layers of evidence of different eras in a city's history, especially in places where dried mud bricks were a popular but not very durable building material. Often, such layered sites include pieces of household odds and ends that had been left behind when a new structure replaced an old one.

These layers help archaeologists read the past. By looking carefully at how deep an artifact is buried and at what lies above and below it, archaeologists can often tell the approximate age of an artifact. They also can compare the artifact with other objects of its kind and determine if it is an earlier or later version of a useful item or an earlier or later style of art. Archaeologists also use scientific methods to test an object's age by measuring the amount of carbon 14 (a radioactive element that disappears with the passage of time) that remains in the materials from which the object is made.

Visitors at the Egyptian Museum in Cairo admire Tutankhamen's gold coffin and other artifacts discovered within his tomb.

Archaeology can be a very slow and tedious business, and archaeologists don't begin work at a site simply by chopping away at the ground with a pick and shovel, as you would if you were digging a ditch. In fact, artifacts from distant ages can be so delicate that much archaeological work is done with tools the size of teaspoons and with soft brushes that can gently whisk away soil.

But why do archaeologists go through all this trouble? Why do they brave hostile climates and dangerous terrain? And why spend endless hours studying the tiniest details of broken things that may well have been thrown away by the people who used them? The answer lies in the fact that all human life is connected, from the earliest days to the present. What we learn about the past helps us understand how we got where we are today and how civilizations might develop in the future. Every culture, no matter how distant from the present, is important. And before anyone else can begin studying the lives of people who lived long ago, archaeologists must read their stories from the artifacts left behind.

Austen Henry Layard (1817-1884), one of the first professional archaeologists, uncovered long-lost palaces that had been home to Assyrians as early as the ninth century B.C.

1

Austen Henry Layard and Hormuzd Rassam
The Legends of Assyria

*B*y the middle of the nineteenth century, Christian and Jewish people had been reading the Bible as the word of God for thousands of years. The Old Testament of the Bible was accepted as an accurate history of the Hebrew people during the centuries between the time of Abraham and the time of Christ. But several other groups of people were mentioned in the Bible and, except for the Egyptians, not much was known about them. Among these groups of people that had been lost to history were the Assyrians, who were described in the Bible and a few other old writings as the rulers of a mighty empire and enemies of the Hebrews. But who were these people? Had they ever really existed or were they simply a people of legend?

With the help of the still-new science of archaeology, these questions about the Assyrians would be answered by the end of the 1800s. Among those who unraveled the mystery of Assyria were Austen Henry Layard of England, and Hormuzd Rassam, a native of Ottoman Mesopotamia (now Iraq).

The Assyrians were the conquerors of the ancient empire of Babylonia, which was centered in the fertile lands between the Tigris and the Euphrates rivers. This region, now a part of Iraq, was once called *Mesopotamia* (from the Greek words meaning "between the rivers"). Assyria had been a province of Babylonia until the Assyrians captured the city of Babylon near the end of the twelfth century B.C.

Two hundred years later, the great age of the Assyrian Empire began. Under three powerful kings—Sargon II, Sennacherib, and Ashurbanipal—the Assyrians were the most feared conquerors of the ancient Middle East. The Assyrians ruled from their proud capital of Nineveh until Assyria's many enemies destroyed the empire in 612 B.C.

Warriors conquered Mesopotamia and the surrounding lands many times over the next 2,500 years, while the dust settled deeply over Nineveh and the other cities of ancient Assyria. The Moslem Arabs, who eventually came to live in the land between the rivers, knew nothing about the lost civilization of ancient Assyria.

By the early 1800s, Mesopotamia had long been a part of the Turkish Empire. Harshly ruled by the Turks and inhabited by people with little trust of foreigners, the region was very dangerous for travelers. One of those travelers was young Austen Henry Layard.

Austen Henry Layard was born to English parents in Paris in 1817. As a child, he frequently traveled in Europe. Even though his parents had little money, they introduced their son (whom they called Henry) to interesting people and taught him about art and literature. As a boy, Henry's favorite book was *The Arabian Nights*, a collection of fantastic stories set in the deserts and palaces of the Middle East. "To them," he later wrote of these stories, "I attribute that love of travel and adventure which took me to the East, and led me to the discovery of the ruins of Nineveh."

Because Henry's parents couldn't afford to send him to college, they sent him to be a clerk in a London law office when he was almost 17. At that time, becoming a law clerk was the first step to becoming an attorney. Although Henry planned to study law, he really wanted to travel.

About six years later, he eventually had a chance to do both. An uncle, who had made a successful career on the island of Ceylon near India, came to London and suggested that Henry go to Ceylon to practice law. Henry liked the idea and soon made plans to travel with another young man, Edward Mitford, who was heading to Ceylon to start a coffee plantation. Because Mitford became seasick on ocean voyages, the two men decided on the far more adventurous land route to India. That was how Austen Henry Layard happened to be traveling on horseback through Mesopotamia in 1839.

Approaching the town of Mosul on the west bank of the Tigris, Austen Henry Layard looked across the broad river to the mounds that—according to local legend—covered the ruins of Nineveh. As he gazed at the great

Although he had planned to become a lawyer, young Austen Henry Layard stumbled into a career in archaeology instead.

heaps of earth, Layard must have wondered why no one had ever made an effort to dig into them and uncover their secrets. In fact, hardly anyone had even scratched their surface. Twenty years earlier, an English official living in Baghdad had visited the mounds. He had taken away a few pieces of sculpture and fragments of clay tablets covered with the triangular symbols called cuneiform writing, which was barely understood at that time. But no real archaeological work had ever been done at the site.

Layard visited not only the Nineveh mounds but also the sites of partly buried ruins at Kalah Shergat, which were 50 miles away, and the mound that legends said covered the ruins of the city of Nimrud. According to legend, Nimrud (or Nimrod) was the great-grandson of the biblical Noah and one of the legendary founders of the Assyrian people. Layard found this mound especially fascinating. It was to Nimrud, which at one point he confused with Nineveh itself, that he most wanted to return.

Layard never got to Ceylon. After an exciting raft trip down the Tigris River to Baghdad and further adventures in Persia, he and Mitford went their separate ways. Mitford continued on to India, while Layard made a roundabout return to Baghdad. Heading back toward Europe, he stopped at the Turkish city of Constantinople. There, he became friendly with the British ambassador, Sir Stratford Canning. Sir Stratford was eager to hear what Layard had learned during his many months among the tribes of Persia and Mesopotamia. But Layard also had plenty to tell about the mounds and ruins of the Tigris Valley, and his desire to discover what they might reveal.

While working for Sir Stratford over the next few years, Layard traveled and gathered information throughout the Turkish Empire. Finally, in 1845, Layard left Constantinople with a special gift from the ambassador: Sir Stratford had given him the money he needed to return to Mesopotamia and hire workers for an archaeological dig. That November, Layard took a boat down the Tigris to the mound of Nimrud.

During the years that Layard was living in Constantinople, work had finally begun on the Assyrian ruins. In 1840, a French archaeologist named Paul Emile Botta began digging at the mound at Khorsabad near Mosul. There he discovered the palace of King Sargon, which had been built near Nineveh in 709 B.C. The sculptures, household articles, and richly carved walls of Sargon's palace finally brought the Assyrian Empire out of the pages of the Bible and into the light of history. Layard was now more determined than ever to unearth more of the Assyrian past at Nimrud.

Arriving at Mosul in the midst of a rebellion against the Turkish governor, Layard immediately set out into the countryside and hired workmen from the sheik who ruled the tribes that lived near Nimrud. On the following morning, November 9, 1845, Layard and his crew began to dig. Few archaeologists—especially in the days when so much guesswork was involved in archaeology—ever met with so much success so soon after starting their excavations. Here is what Layard wrote to Sir Stratford Canning about that first day at Nimrud:

> Having opened a trench in a part of the mound in which a block of stone projected from the ground I came at once upon a chamber 25 feet long and 14 broad, formed by slabs of marble 8 1/2 feet in length, each slab containing an inscription in the cuneiform character! I opened one part of the chamber to the flooring, which I found to be of marble and covered with inscriptions.

The room Layard had found was part of the palace of King Ashurnasirpal II, who had reigned from 883 to 859 B.C. In the palace were small statues made of ivory that still showed traces of gold trim. Although this was a significant discovery in itself, on that same day Layard uncovered a second palace. Built 200 years later by a king named Esarhaddon, this second palace contained wonderful examples of sculptures called *bas reliefs*. The Assyrians were among history's great masters of this type of sculpture. Layard marveled (as museum-goers have marveled in the 150 years since then) at the lively figures, which seemed almost to leap out of the Assyrian reliefs; in some of these sculptures, horses and chariots look as if

"Attendant to the King" is one of several bas reliefs
found within the palace of Ashurnasirpal II, which
was built at Nimrud between 883 and 859 B.C.

they are ready to turn from their flat surfaces and gallop toward the viewer.

When most people think of Assyrian sculpture, though, they tend to think of the huge, winged bodies, lions, horses, and bulls (which often had the heads of men) that stood guard at palaces and temples. Layard found these types of sculptures as well—13 pairs of them. The archaeologist sent two of the giant sculptures—a bull and a lion—to England. It took more than 300 men to drag them by cart to a river raft, on which they were floated down the Tigris River to the Persian Gulf. Today, they stand in the British Museum in London.

After making these major finds, Layard caught the full fever of archaeology. As he wrote his aunt, "I live among the ruins, and dream of little else." But his greatest achievement lay ahead.

In 1847, Layard turned his attention to the first Assyrian mounds he had seen, the ones across the Tigris from Mosul that people believed were covering the ruins of Nineveh. (He no longer had to worry about money because his work was being paid by the British Museum.) Layard began by digging straight down into the mound called Kuyunjik, which French archaeologist Paul Botta had already attempted to excavate without any success. But Layard was much more fortunate than Botta had been. After running into a layer of brickwork 20 feet down, Layard told his men to dig off to the sides in several directions. One of them discovered a gate that was guarded by a pair of great winged bulls.

Layard now directed all of their efforts at the area behind the gate. After almost a month of hard work, the diggers unearthed nine more rooms. Layard had found nothing less than the palace of Sennacherib, who had called Nineveh "my royal city" and raised it to its greatest heights of glory.

Sennacherib, who reigned from 705 to 681 B.C., was one of the fiercest rulers of the ancient world. He warred almost constantly with his neighbors and hated Babylon with such fury that after conquering the city, he killed all of its inhabitants and flooded its ruined streets with the waters of the Tigris. His greatest defeat was at the walls of Jerusalem, where his army fell sick with malaria.

But Sennacherib was also a great builder, and Henry Layard was viewing one of his greatest works. The palace had more than 70 rooms, and nearly 10,000 feet of bas reliefs lined its walls. Most interesting of all, though, was a part of the palace that had nothing to do with the life of vanity and military conquest lived by Sennacherib. One pair of rooms were filled with clay tablet "books" that had been collected by his more peaceable grandson, Ashurbanipal, one of the last kings of Assyria before the destruction of Nineveh.

The 25,000 tablets kept in those two rooms made up one of the oldest libraries ever discovered. The massive library had been assembled when Ashurbanipal ordered

Like other bas reliefs found in the palace of Ashurnasirpal II, "Genie with Pail and Date-Palm Spathe" is nearly ten feet tall.

that every bit of written information in the known world be brought to him and copied by his scribes in cuneiform. The collection included works of history, medicine, science, and literature. Much of the work of excavating and organizing Ashurbanipal's library of clay tablets was done by one of Layard's assistants, a young man named Hormuzd Rassam.

Hormuzd Rassam was a native of Mosul, Ottoman Mesopotamia. Born in 1826, he was a member of a Christian Arab group known as Chaldeans. Because his brother was an official with the British government, Hormuzd Rassam was able to go to Oxford University. Even before his college days in England, however, he had helped Layard with the dig at Nimrud.

Years later, Rassam would work as an archaeologist in charge of his own projects. It was a welcome change for a descendant of the ancient cultures of the Middle East to begin excavating on his own instead of merely serving as a digger or foreman for a European archaeologist. Among Rassam's later discoveries was a temple at Balawat, north of Nimrud. This temple, built by an earlier Assyrian king named Ashurnasirpal, was part of a vast terraced city. A gate to one of the city's palaces was more than 20 feet high, with a double door made of bronze. This was the first door found anywhere in the ruins of Assyria.

Rassam is probably best remembered, though, for his early discoveries of the clay tablets in the library of

Unlike some archaeologists who traveled across the globe to make their finds, Hormuzd Rassam (1826-1910) of Ottoman Mesopotamia (now Iraq) did most of his archaeological work in his homeland.

Ashurbanipal. Neither Rassam nor Layard could read the tablets because the strange, wedge-shaped cuneiform script was barely understood at the time of their discovery. But 25 years later, in 1872, a self-trained scholar named George Smith finally puzzled out a translation of Ashurbanipal's tablets and the world soon learned the importance of Rassam's finds. The tablets chronicled the adventures of a legendary hero named Gilgamesh and told the creation myth of the Babylonian and Assyrian people.

Smith traveled to nearby Kuyunjik to uncover more of the missing tablets, which were far more interesting and important than most fables. The 3,000-line *Epic of Gilgamesh* contained a flood story almost identical to the account of Noah in the Bible. Both stories described the flood as a punishment, the survival of one man and his family who took animals with them on an ark, and the final grounding of the ark on a mountaintop.

It is not necessary to believe in the Bible to understand the importance of the Gilgamesh discovery. Scholars of all religious beliefs were amazed that there were two accounts from different cultures that said so many of the same things about the early days of civilized humankind. For centuries, Europeans had wondered if the Bible had included the truth about the Assyrians. And here was an Assyrian account of an even more ancient story that matched one in the Bible. (The *Epic of Gilgamesh* was written 2,000 years before the Bible.)

According to the Bible, Noah, his family, and one pair of every animal survived a powerful flood by living for several months inside a gigantic ark.

Gilgamesh, an impetuous hero in Babylonian mythology, was allegedly descended from Utnapishtim and his wife—the only two survivors of a flood.

Whether there really had been a terrible flood, or whether the peoples of Israel and Mesopotamia had dreamed the same dreams about their origins, it is now evident that these ancient societies had common bonds.

After the discovery of the Gilgamesh tablets, Hormuzd Rassam's reputation as an archaeologist grew. Austen Henry Layard, meanwhile, entered the world of government as a British politician and ambassador. In his later life, Layard may have enjoyed thinking that these discoveries came about because of his own adventurous spirit, his love of *The Arabian Nights*—and the fact that a friend had once worried about becoming seasick on the ship to Ceylon.

Although the archaeological career of Henri Mouhot (1826-1861) was brief, his discovery of the remains of the Khmer Empire created work for many archaeologists who succeeded him.

2

Henri Mouhot
The Temple of Angkor

*T*ime often works upon the memory of great empires in the same way that jungle vines work upon abandoned cities. With the passage of a few hundred years, the world can forget that a once-powerful civilization had ever existed. This is what happened to the empire of the Khmer, who ruled over much of Southeast Asia from their capital in the land of present-day Cambodia. The name of that capital was Angkor. The Khmer abandoned it when invaders from Siam (now Thailand) conquered their empire in the mid-1400s, and it remained lost and forgotten in the jungle until the year 1860.

The Cambodian peasants who, by the 1800s, were a far less powerful people than their ancestors had been, knew of the great sandstone buildings in the jungle north of the Tonle Sap lake. But they had no idea who had built the ruined, vine-covered temples and monuments. Indeed, they couldn't imagine anyone building such structures. Gods built them, they said, and some even claimed that the buildings of Angkor had built themselves.

Angkor was one of those places that sounded so fantastic to the Western world that for a long time almost no one believed Angkor actually existed. As early as the mid-1500s, when the Khmer capital had been abandoned for only 100 years, a Portuguese missionary had brought home a tale of a "forest of huge and terrifying ruins of palaces, halls, and temples." Over the centuries, other missionaries and travelers told similar stories. In the 1850s, several English adventurers wrote or spoke of having seen the mysterious Cambodian ruins. But the world never seemed to pay attention, as if nothing so vast and strange could be real.

Ironically, the man who finally discovered Angkor was not even a trained archaeologist. He was Henri Mouhot, a young French naturalist who had come to Cambodia in 1859 to collect specimens of tropical plants. The following year, in a town not far from the Tonle Sap lake, a missionary priest told Mouhot about the ruins that were supposed to be hidden in the jungle. The missionary suggested that they both try to find the lost city. Mouhot agreed, and the two men set off for Angkor.

The trip was long and dangerous, even though the distance to be covered would have been only 50 miles if they had been able to travel in a straight line. But no straight-line routes existed in the jungle. At first, Mouhot and the priest, accompanied by local guides and drivers, traveled by carriages pulled by water buffaloes. Again and again, the carriages sank up to their axles in swamp mud, and the drivers had to cut away fallen trees that blocked the crude road. Finally, the men reached Tonle Sap and crossed it by canoe. Near the northern end of the giant lake they paddled into a small stream, which they followed northward into the jungle. Sometimes, the stream became too shallow or too rough, and they had to get out of the canoe and walk.

After nearly a month of slow, hard travel, Mouhot's patience and toughness were rewarded. Emerging from the jungle, he and his companions stood at the entrance to a long and straight stone-paved roadway that led across a wide moat. Half a mile ahead of them stood what was probably the largest temple in the world: Angkor Wat. (The word *wat* means temple.)

The moat facing Mouhot was 200 yards across and nearly a mile along each side. At the center of the great square island, walls large enough to enclose nearly nine football fields surrounded the central temple, which had

Angkor Wat was the only structure in Angkor undamaged by the passage of time.

five towers shaped like blossoms of the lotus flower. The central tower was more than 200 feet tall and was surrounded by magnificent wall carvings of graceful dancers and gold statues of Hindu gods. The Khmer had once worshiped their king himself as a god.

Henri Mouhot could hardly believe his eyes. "It is grander than anything left to us by Greece or Rome," he later wrote. But he had only begun to explore the mysteries of Angkor. Two miles north of the temple, he found a road overgrown with jungle vegetation that led to the gates of a great walled city. This was Angkor Thom, the second capital of the Khmer. Within these walls and scattered through the jungle outside of them over an area of more than 40 square miles, stood the ruins of hundreds of temples, monuments, and other buildings.

Because Buddhist monks were still using Angkor Wat as a place for prayer (Buddhism had followed Hinduism to Cambodia), the huge building and its walls had been kept in fairly good condition. But this was not true of the rest of Angkor. The jungle vegetation had not been kind to the old Khmer metropolis. Everywhere Mouhot looked, he found walls broken and huge building stones cast about as if giants had kicked the city apart. Trees had grown in rooms and courtyards, and pushed their way through roofs.

The banyan trees, called "strangling figs," had done the most damage of all. Their enormous, above-ground

Angkor Wat, possibly the largest religious structure in the world, continued to stand more than 700 years after it was built.

roots had pried and tugged at the buildings of Angkor, pulling apart stones until walls and towers had toppled. Here and there, pieces of broken statues rose from the jungle floor. To the young Frenchman, who wrote that he could hear the roar of tigers and the trumpeting of elephants amidst the deep shadows of the surrounding forests, Angkor must have seemed like the loneliest place on earth.

Mouhot spent three weeks at Angkor, measuring, sketching, and taking notes. But no matter how hard he tried to understand what he saw, he had no idea who had built the monuments or how long they had stood forgotten in the jungle. He decided that the ruins must be at least 2,000 years old and that they were the work of an unknown and vanished people. He believed the ancestors of the present-day Cambodians could not have built Angkor because Cambodia was a nation composed largely of poor rice farmers.

Henri Mouhot would never learn the answer to the mystery of Angkor. In the autumn of 1861, he died of a tropical fever in the jungles of Laos. Mouhot had his Angkor notebooks with him at the time of his death, however, and his servants brought the notes back to civilization. Within three years, Mouhot's notes were published in French and British journals. Although he was no longer alive, Mouhot had done something the earlier visitors to Angkor had not been able to accomplish. He had made people believe in the wonders he had seen.

Henri Mouhot, however, was incorrect in his two primary assumptions about Angkor. First, the city had been built around A.D. 1100—far more recently than he had thought. In fact, it had been abandoned for only 400 years when he had first come upon it. Second, it was, indeed, the work of ancestors of the same people whom Mouhot had watched tend their rice fields and water buffaloes. During the late 1800s, in the decades following Mouhot's death, French and Dutch scholars studied the writings on the walls of Angkor and compared them with other records of bygone times in southeast Asia.

The story of Cambodian civilization began about 2,000 years ago (the time Mouhot mistakenly thought Angkor had been built), when traders from India brought their Hindu religion to the southern parts of the Indochinese Peninsula. The Khmer, who adopted the Hindu religion, had originally come from the mountains in the north of Cambodia.

By the first century A.D., the Khmer ruled a kingdom of their own, which reached over much of the peninsula. The great days of Khmer civilization, however, began around A.D. 800. That year, a king named Jayavarman II began a struggle to unite Cambodia and free it from the rule of Java, an island to the south. Jayavarman II was successful and ruled for nearly 50 years. During this time, he made himself the center of the Khmer religion— an all-powerful "god-king." This belief would last for the next 600 years of the Khmer Empire.

The walled city of Angkor Thom, built about A.D. 1171, lay mostly in ruins by the mid-1800s—grown over with vegetation.

Jayavarman did not build Angkor, however. His descendant Yasovarman, who became king in 899, began building the great city. Once Yasovarman had decided on the site for his new capital, he set his slaves to building temples, palaces, walls, and reservoirs. The work went on for hundreds of years until Angkor was a great city where kings and princes rode on the backs of elephants through magnificent gateways, and grand displays of fireworks marked the beginning of each new year. In the early years of the twelfth century, the powerful King Suryavarman II ordered the building of the city's greatest monument, Angkor Wat. By the end of that century, Jayavarman VII built the walled city of Angkor Thom.

Some historians believe that the enormous cost of these great building projects helped lead to the ruin of the Khmer Empire. That may be so, but the Khmer also had many enemies. During the early 1400s, invaders from Siam attacked Angkor. When the Siamese returned two years later, they discovered that the once-proud city had been abandoned.

Where had the Khmer of Angkor gone? Many had eventually settled at Phnom Penh, which is the capital of modern Cambodia. But the Khmer kingdom was never to regain its old power and glory. For 400 years after Angkor's fall, Cambodia was pressed constantly between two strong neighbors, Siam (now Thailand) and Vietnam. In the 1860s, shortly after Mouhot's travels, the land of the Khmer came under the control of the French government, as did Vietnam and Laos. All through those troubled centuries, the place of mystery and rumor called Angkor was left to decay in the jungle.

When Henri Mouhot's notes were published as a book after his death, French historians and archaeologists immediately became interested in this wonderful place discovered in a far corner of the French Empire. Soon, French historians and archaeologists organized expeditions to study the lost city more carefully. They cleared the jungle growth from its ruins and planned ways to repair the buildings so they would not decay even more.

For nearly 100 years, scholars, engineers, and laborers toiled to learn about and restore Angkor. They hacked away trees and vines, and they read and translated old inscriptions to learn the city's history. They also installed drainpipes so water would not destroy the soft sandstone of the buildings. Most amazing of all, the French engineers and archaeologists actually rebuilt many of the monuments from the stones scattered across the jungle, putting them back together like a giant jigsaw puzzle. Because of their hard work, buildings like the Bayon Temple, with its 54 towers, soar into the jungle canopy. Once again, thousands of carved dancers—called *apsaras*—spring gracefully to life from temple walls.

Sadly, the worst period in Cambodian history since the fall of the Khmer interrupted the century-long job of restoring Angkor. From the 1960s to the 1980s, the

By the end of the nineteenth century, the French began repairing many buildings at Angkor, which had been abandoned for more than 400 years.

country suffered a bloody civil war, an oppressive government, and a Vietnamese invasion. When its caretakers left for safety, Angkor was left to the jungle once again. At times, soldiers even hid among the ruins and shot at the lovely statues just for fun.

In the future, peace may return to Cambodia. When that happens, work can begin again on preserving the great capital that was for so long lost to everyone and to everything but time itself.

A book he read as a child inspired Heinrich Schliemann (1822-1890) to study the distant past.

3

Heinrich Schliemann
The Walls of Troy

*O*ne of the oldest and best-loved stories ever told is the *Iliad*. Written by the Greek poet Homer around the year 750 B.C., the *Iliad* is a tale of bravery, anger, and revenge during a long war between Greece and the city-state of Troy. The Trojan War, as this conflict is now called, was already several centuries in the past by the time Homer spoke the words of his masterpiece. (At that time, poets composed their verses to be read aloud.)

Historians now know a great deal about the Greeks, who created a society that became one of the foundations of European civilization. But what about Troy? Did this enemy of Greece really exist, or was the story of the Trojan War merely a poet's fantasy? If there was a Troy, where was it located? During the early 1870s, these questions fascinated a German businessman named Heinrich Schliemann. While trying to find the answer to this puzzle, Schliemann became one of the leaders of modern archaeology.

Heinrich Schliemann was born in 1822 in the town of Neubukow in northern Germany. His father was the pastor of a Protestant church, and the family was poor. But one thing that brightened Heinrich's childhood was his father's practice of telling legends and stories from history. Even if he could not afford to send his son to fine schools, Pastor Schliemann wanted Heinrich to have a scholar's curiosity about the world. On Christmas Day, 1829, he gave Heinrich an illustrated book of world history, and it was to give the boy a lifelong dream.

As Heinrich looked at the artist's drawings of the great events of history, one picture caught his imagination more than any other. It showed the Greeks burning the city of Troy during the Trojan War and the collapse of the city's great walls. Heinrich's father had told him Homer's stories from the *Iliad*, and the picture of the fall of Troy—even if it was only an artist's imagined version—had filled him with wonder. He told his father that if Troy had been encircled by walls that large, surely

The Greek poet Homer is best remembered for composing the Iliad, *which is still widely read more than 2,700 years later.*

something must be left of them. When he grew up, Heinrich declared, he would go and find them.

That was far more easily said than done. At that time, no one went to school to become an archaeologist. (Archaeology was still a relatively new discipline during the 1800s.) Even if such a course of study had been available, Heinrich Schliemann couldn't afford to attend college. Likewise, since historians were still not even sure if the Trojan War had really happened or where the place called Troy might be located, young Heinrich might as well have decided to go to the moon.

What he did do, however, was go to work. Putting aside the dreams that had grown out of picture books and fireside tales, Heinrich Schliemann took a job in a grocery store at the age of 14. He had all the schooling his father could afford and did not receive a formal education until he was a middle-aged man.

Hard work, luck, and an amazing ability to learn languages made Schliemann wealthy while he was still quite young. The grocery store didn't hold him for long. After the ship that was supposed to take him to South America was destroyed, Schliemann went to Holland instead. There he learned bookkeeping and taught himself Russian. Then, Schliemann moved to the Russian city of St. Petersburg, where he set up his own business as an import-export broker—someone who buys and sells goods that are shipped from one country to another.

Schliemann was only 28 years old and already wealthy when he sailed to the United States. As a buyer of gold dust during the California gold rush, Schliemann grew even richer. (He had already taught himself English, along with most of the European languages.) Returning to Russia and his import-export business, Schliemann piled up an ever-greater fortune. In 1863, though, he decided that his years of money-making were over. He was only 41 years old and was worth tens of millions of dollars. From there on, he promised himself, he would spend his life exploring the mysteries of the ancient Greek world, especially the story of Troy. In his heart, he was still a little boy fascinated by a picture book.

By now, Schliemann could read ancient Greek, the language of Homer. He had read the *Iliad* over and over, so many times that he was familiar with every clue that the long poem contained about the appearance of the Trojan landscape. Toward the end of his business career and into his retirement, Schliemann spent four years not only studying the *Iliad* and Homer's *Odyssey*, but also reading everything he could find that had survived from the ancient Greeks. He even taught himself to write in the old language, boasting that if it were possible, he could send a letter to someone in ancient Greece and have it understood.

Schliemann even put in two years of study at a university, something poverty had kept him from doing as a young man. At the Sorbonne in Paris, he took courses in archaeology and in the history of the lands that lay at the eastern end of the Mediterranean Sea—the lands that formed the setting of the *Iliad*.

In the summer of 1868, Schliemann set off for Greece. After digging on the island of Ithaca, where Ulysses (the hero of the *Odyssey*) had ended his long journey, the self-made archaeologist sailed for the lands of the *Iliad*.

The scholars who believed that the Trojan War had actually happened thought the site of Troy must be on the western shores of the peninsula now occupied by the country of Turkey. This area, called Asia Minor in ancient times, lay directly across the Aegean Sea from

Greece and its many islands. But when Schliemann reached the little Turkish village that scholars usually thought was the closest modern town to the vanished old fortress-city, he knew something was wrong. The place just didn't fit Homer's descriptions, which Schliemann considered as authentic as a contemporary travel guide.

Schliemann felt much better about a place farther north, the town Hissarlik. Hissarlik was near the coast, which was important because Homer had told how the Greeks moved easily between their ships and the walls of Troy. The site Schliemann chose also looked promising because it was in the shape of a great, flat-topped mound, over 700 feet on each side. According to Homer, the enormous palace of Troy, which housed more than 50 rooms, sat atop just such a plateau. It was exactly the kind of site that could have been defended by the enormous walls described in the *Iliad* and pictured in the book Schliemann had received on that long-ago Christmas. Satisfied that he was close to his lifelong goal, he began his dig in April of 1870.

Sixteen feet below the surface, Schliemann's Turkish workers struck the remains of a huge wall more than six feet thick. Schliemann, who was prone to jump to premature conclusions, immediately declared that this wall and the deeper wall on which it rested must be part of the defenses of Troy. In his notebook, he even wrote that the ancient stones might be part of the palace of Priam, the Trojan king. (According to legend, Priam's son, Paris, had prompted the Trojan War by kidnapping Helen, who was married to the king of the Greek city-state of Sparta.) As Schliemann's picks and shovels bit into the Turkish earth, all scenes from the *Iliad*, which he knew so well, must have raced through his mind.

It would have been an amazing stroke of luck if Schliemann had actually found the walls of Troy or the ruins of Priam's palace on this first dig at Hissarlik. But he had not. Schliemann had no way of knowing that he had struck only the latest of a long series of towns and fortresses that ancient people had built on this site over thousands of years. This topmost "Troy" was the remains of a settlement called New Ilium, or Ilion, which was itself more than 2,500 years old. The excited German excavator lost no time, however, in telling the world that he had found the ruins of Homer's Troy.

Over the following year, Schliemann began to learn that perhaps he had spoken too soon. Because of a disagreement with the Turkish government over permission for his dig, he had had to stop his work soon after he had begun. But in October 1871, he returned with the proper permissions and continued where he had left off. Up to 150 workers at a time sweated over picks and shovels as they made their way deeper and deeper into the great mound of Hissarlik. As they delved, Schliemann realized his mistake of the previous year. The ruins closest to the surface were from the Roman Era (27 to 395 A.D.), not from the earlier times of ancient Greece.

By the time the coming winter forced them to stop digging, Schliemann's crews had shoveled through so many layers of human settlement that the archaeologist was both surprised and confused. They had dug to a level where the artifacts all belonged to people of the Stone Age (approximately 40,000 to 6000 B.C.), the time before humans began using metal. And yet Schliemann knew that the warriors of Troy and Greece had used metal swords and helmets and that they possessed ships and chariots and fine golden ornaments. Surely they were not primitive Stone-Age men.

Schliemann decided to keep on digging. He excavated a huge trench across the mound of Hissarlik until he had uncovered as much as possible of each level of settlement. He returned to Hissarlik in 1872 and again in 1873. That year, he found a treasure of gold jewelry— thousands of beautifully made earrings, rings, bracelets, and other precious objects, which he believed to have belonged to King Priam himself.

The treasure had been buried two levels up from the bare earth at the bottom of the Hissarlik mound, near the ruins of a large building that Schliemann called "Priam's palace"—the same name he had given to his first find in 1870. He even found the remains of a wide gate, which he declared to be the very gate the Greeks had used to enter the city by surprise while hidden inside their gigantic wooden horse. (The expression "Trojan Horse" is now used to describe something that looks harmless but contains danger within.)

54

According to legend, Greek invaders surprised the Trojans by giving them a gigantic wooden horse that secretly held soldiers inside.

By 1873, Schliemann was satisfied that he had found Troy. Homer had described the burning of the city in the *Iliad*, and both the second and third levels from the bottom showed the marks of a terrible fire. Schliemann was sure the fire-scars on the ruins of the second level were made by the flames he had seen pictured in his Christmas book.

Looking back, Schliemann had once more been hasty in saying for certain that he had found the Troy of the *Iliad*, with its walls and gates, palace, and treasure. Because he wanted to find these things so badly, Schliemann convinced himself he *had* found them, no matter how incomplete the evidence. After all, Schliemann reasoned, no one else had even bothered to dig at Hissarlik or had thought to use Homer as a guide, and no one could say who the artifacts Schliemann had found belonged to, if not to the Trojans.

All of this did not stop university scholars from ridiculing Schliemann and his work, especially after his story was published in his 1875 book, *Troy and Its Remains*. Schliemann was a mere businessman without a professor's title, the critics complained. They called him a treasure-hunter, and some even said he was a fraud who had found his treasure in a secondhand shop. Deep down, many of these historians—some of whom had never seen an archaeological dig—were upset that someone had tried to tie a great work of literature to the actual past.

A large wall surrounded the ancient city-state of Troy, which was located near the modern town of Hissarlik, Turkey.

As an archaeologist, Schliemann's fault was being overly enthusiastic. He was careless with any discoveries that did not have to do with his great goal. While digging through the layers of settlement that led to Homer's Troy, he thoughtlessly tossed aside pieces of pottery and smashed through ruins that could have provided significant information about other periods of history. As he grew older, he recognized these mistakes. Eventually, archaeology would become such a precise field of study that archaeologists would not ignore or throw away even the tiniest artifact.

Heinrich Schliemann also worked at many other sites in the lands of the ancient Greeks. The most important of these was Mycenae, where he discovered the tombs of kings who had been buried in golden masks and armor. One of them, Schliemann claimed, was none other than Agamemnon, leader of the Greek forces that fought before the walls of Troy. To this day, no one can say for certain that it was.

It was Troy, though, that fascinated Schliemann for the rest of his life. He returned to the vast dig at Hissarlik in 1878, 1882, and again in 1890. That year, he started a new excavation with a fellow archaeologist, Wilhelm Dörpfeld. Dörpfeld made a careful study of the historical order of each level of settlement and made a good estimate of the age of each. The level of "Priam's treasure," he discovered, dated back much further than the events of the *Iliad*. The Troy of Homer's poem was the seventh of

This drawing shows Heinrich Schliemann sketching the ruins of Troy.

nine levels—only two levels from the top surface. Schliemann had discovered it, all right, and then had passed it while digging farther down.

Dörpfeld came to this final conclusion in 1894, but Schliemann was not alive to share it. He had died four years earlier on December 25, 1890—exactly 61 years after he had opened a special Christmas present that would spark his lifelong mission.

*The archaeological work of Sir Arthur Evans
(1851-1941) on the island of Crete helped to show
that sometimes myths have a basis in reality.*

4

Sir Arthur Evans
Knossos and the Minotaur

*O*ne of the most exciting and terrifying of all Greek myths was the tale of King Minos, who reigned on the eastern Mediterranean island of Crete. After the king of Athens killed Minos's son, Minos imposed a harsh punishment on the Greek city-state of Athens. Every nine years, Minos forced Athens to send seven young men and seven young women to the palace at Knossos on Crete. There, King Minos sent the youths into a giant maze called the Labyrinth, where they would lose their way and be eaten by the horrible Minotaur—a monster with the body of a man and the head of a bull.

The legend tells of a brave young man named Theseus, who traveled from Athens and volunteered to become part of the group to be sacrificed to the Minotaur. Theseus fell in love with Minos's daughter, Ariadne. She gave Theseus a magical spool of thread as he was about to enter the Labyrinth. In order to retrace his steps, he left one end of the thread at the entrance to the Labyrinth and unravelled the spool as he walked through the confusing tunnels. When Theseus reached the heart of the maze, he killed the Minotaur. Then, following the thread, Theseus led his companions to daylight and safety.

The Minotaur—one of the most ferocious creatures in Greek mythology—hunted, killed, and ate the young men and women trapped in his deadly Labyrinth.

The Minotaur was a mythological creature, of course. But legends often have some basis in truth, even if the facts only go as far as the names of the people and places involved. Who was Minos, and where was his capital of Knossos? Was there really an advanced civilization on Crete, older and at one time more powerful than the mainland states of classical Greece? The work of unearthing this lost civilization, called the Minoan Kingdom (named after King Minos), was done by an English archaeologist named Sir Arthur Evans. Through Evans's 25 years of patient excavation and reconstruction, the modern world came to know this early European society.

Just as experts had once dismissed the existence of the city of Troy, scholars had long believed that the cities of ancient Crete belonged only to the realm of myth and legend. Until archaeology became an established science during the late nineteenth century, most experts believed that historians and archaeologists could not accurately trace the history of the Mediterranean world beyond the eighth century B.C., the time of the earliest Greek writings.

Scholars now know that the Minoan civilization had risen and fallen long before Greek was a written language. (The Minoans' own hieroglyphic type of writing is still not completely understood today.) Human settlement on Crete, in fact, dates back at least 8,000 years, much further back than the time of the earliest Egyptian pharaohs.

The earliest known inhabitants of Crete were primitive farmers of the period known as the New Stone Age (approximately 8000 to 6000 B.C.). No one knows for sure how they reached the island—whether they came from the mainland of Europe or from Asia Minor (the location of present-day Turkey). By the time of the Bronze Age, when people began to learn how to use this metal made from copper and tin (approximately 2800 to 2600 B.C.), more immigrants from Asia Minor and possibly North Africa, joined these early Cretans. Civilization on the island became more advanced and reached its peak 1,000 years later with the luxurious cities and palaces of the Minoans—and then mysteriously disappeared, giving birth to the mystery of Minos.

Arthur Evans first visited Crete in 1894. Then 43 years old, he was a wealthy scholar in charge of the Ashmolean Museum at England's Oxford University. His father, John Evans, was himself an amateur archaeologist with a special interest in the ancient history of the British Isles. Arthur Evans had come to Crete to study the unknown language carved on small stones found there. Before long, though, he decided to look beyond the writings and actually to begin excavations at Knossos.

Knossos and its palace were not entirely forgotten. As long ago as the time of the Roman Empire—when the Golden Age of the Minoans was already more than

1,500 years in the past—writers spoke of the ruins at Knossos. In the seventeenth century A.D., an English author claimed he had seen the entrance to the Labyrinth. He hadn't, but his supposed location wasn't very far from Knossos. In 1878, an amateur Greek archaeologist began digging at the site of Knossos and uncovered parts of an ancient building. American writer William James Stillman came up with a theory that these ruins might have something to do with the Labyrinth. Archaeologist Heinrich Schliemann himself wanted to dig there, as he had done so successfully at Troy, but he could not come to terms with the Turkish owners of the site. The next move belonged to Arthur Evans, who purchased the area above Knossos in 1900 and immediately started digging.

One year later, Evans said he would need another year to finish the excavations. Little did he know that he would be digging until 1932. (He was interrupted by the First World War in 1914 and did not continue until 1922.) Evans had, after all, begun unearthing a palace that covered five and one-half acres—a building as large as Buckingham Palace, the royal residence in London. In addition to the palace, he discovered many other structures that stood at the center of Minos's glorious capital.

During the first months of digging, Evans and his crews uncovered the west wing of the palace. As the years wore on, he excavated the east wing on the opposite side of a great central courtyard, as well as palace living quarters, separate houses for government officials, and storerooms so vast they could hold 19,000 gallons of liquid. The archaeologist learned that the Minoans of 3,500 years ago had a surprisingly modern plumbing system, with toilets that could be flushed with water—things unheard of in Europe until well into the nineteenth century. Evans even found the throne room of King Minos, with a simple but majestic throne carved from gypsum— probably the oldest such royal chair ever found in Europe. (No one is sure whether there actually was a single individual named "King Minos" or if "minos" was a royal title like "pharaoh" or "caesar.")

Throughout the palace, Evans discovered beautifully decorated pottery, figurines of carved ivory, and walls covered with vivid paintings and frescoes. (When creating a fresco, the artist applies paint to plaster that is still wet.) As he proceeded, Evans worked with an architect and a painter to restore and repaint the walls, stairways, and columns he uncovered.

Many scholars now feel that the colors and restorations might have depended too much on guesswork. But when visitors enter the rooms of Knossos today, they feel like they are walking through the halls and chambers of a real palace, and not merely a crumbling ruin. The bright colors and sunny, open feeling of the rooms around the light-giving central courtyard also remind us that this was a palace, not a gloomy fort. It was not fortress walls that had kept the Minoans secure. Rather, a powerful

*From his throne room in the palace of Knossos,
shown here from two different angles, King Minos
ruled over the island of Crete.*

Arthur Evans and his archaeological crews found numerous pieces of pottery in the palace of Knossos, which was destroyed around 1375 B.C.

navy guarding the approaches to the island and protecting its trading vessels served as the Minoans' primary defense.

Perhaps the most interesting element about the vast building that Evans uncovered, though, was the complicated, mazelike pattern of dozens upon dozens of rooms, stairways, halls, and courtyards. The palace at Knossos seemed incredibly similar to the Labyrinth of Greek mythology. It certainly could have been the inspiration for stories of a Labyrinth. Any stranger to the court of Minos could easily have been confused and overwhelmed by the sheer size of the palace and the arrangement of its

*Arthur Evans (in white suit and pith helmet)
and his archaeological team repair the grand
staircase in the Knossos palace around 1905.*

rooms, even if there was no man with the head of a bull roaming inside its walls.

And what about the Minotaur? Perhaps the answer lay with the many paintings and sculptures of bulls that Evans found at Knossos. It is also clear that the bull must have played a great role in Minoan religion and ritual. Like many other early people, the Minoans saw this animal as a symbol of strength. The Minoans sacrificed bulls as part of their religious rites. Additionally, young men and women played dangerous games with bulls, grabbing them by the horns and turning somersaults over their backs. The sacrifices and the daredevil acrobatics involving bulls resemble the ritual of bullfighting that survives to this day in Spain.

Everyone knows that stories change as they are passed from one person to another. Imagine how much different a story can become when it is not only passed down over time but also from one culture to another. It isn't hard to see how the Greeks could eventually tell tales of a vast and complicated palace and of young people risking their lives in dangerous rituals involving bulls; it isn't hard to image those tales turning into the myth of Minos, Theseus, and the Minotaur.

The greatest mystery of Minoan civilization is not the story of the Minotaur, however, but the question of how this rich, comfortable society came to an end. Throughout the years, scholars have offered two main explanations for the sudden decline and disappearance of the Minoans. One theory says that invaders from the European mainland swept across the 60 miles separating Crete from Greece and overthrew the Minoan kings.

A second theory depends upon an even more sudden and exciting event. Around 1500 B.C., one of the greatest volcanic explosions in human history took place on the small island of Thera, which lies between Greece and Crete. With an unimaginable roar, Thera's volcano blew itself apart, sending 20 cubic miles of stone, dust, and lava into the air, causing enormous tidal waves in the sea.

When a volcanic explosion of such magnitude occurs on an island in the sea, the result is an immense

Although he began his archaeological career late in life, Arthur Evans became one of the best-known archaeologists of the nineteenth and twentieth centuries.

tidal wave. The huge wave, combined with the fall of thousands of tons of ash from the darkened sky and the shaking of the earth as Thera exploded, must have dealt the Minoan capital a terrible blow. The islands of Thera and Crete, after all, are less than 70 miles apart.

Arthur Evans himself came to believe that Thera caused the ruin of Knossos. One summer night in 1926, the 75-year-old archaeologist was reading in bed in his house near Knossos when a massive earth tremor nearly tossed him to the floor. When he learned of the great damage the quake had caused in local villages, he quickly decided that a powerful earthquake—similar to the one that may have accompanied the explosion of Thera— could have toppled the buildings of old Knossos.

Today, many historians and archaeologists believe the Minoan Kingdom fell because of a combination of the Thera explosion and an invasion from the mainland. The natural disaster, they reason, upset Minoan society to such an extent that the conquerors' work was easy.

Archaeologists may never discover just what force or combination of forces brought about the ruin of the sophisticated society that surrounded the palace at Knossos. But the idea that terrible natural forces spelled the end of Minoan civilization may have inspired the old and fascinating legend of Atlantis, the "lost continent" that supposedly sank beneath the sea. The legend of Atlantis began in the writings of the Greek philosopher Plato, who lived more than 1,000 years after the fall of

Greek philosopher Plato wrote about the lost continent of Atlantis around the year 400 B.C., and Atlantis—now the subject of numerous films and science-fiction stories—has remained a popular legend ever since.

Knossos. Many writers have suggested that Plato got his idea of a great disaster dooming an advanced civilization from the stories he had heard about Thera and the Minoans.

Who can say what Plato was thinking of when he wrote of his lost continent? Even though it was far smaller than a continent, the Cretan city that Arthur Evans found had surely been lost—and it had been a marvelous place.

*Historian Edward Thompson (1840-1935), who
developed a method for performing underwater
archaeological research, made a chilling discovery
about the Mayan civilization at Chichén Itzá.*

5

Edward Thompson
The Sacred Well at Chichén Itzá

*W*hen people look back on the Spanish conquest of Mexico and Central America during the early years of the sixteenth century, they often think of the swift victory of Hernán Cortés over the mighty Aztec Empire and its ruler, Montezuma. Montezuma's capital stood near the site of the region's largest modern metropolis, Mexico City. For many people, the Aztecs came to symbolize the pre-European history of this land.

But there was another great people of Central America—a people whose civilization had already passed through its Golden Era and into decline by the time the Spanish arrived. The descendants of these people are the native inhabitants of Guatemala and southeastern Mexico, including the Yucatán Peninsula. They were the Maya, and in the days of their glory, they were the most advanced society in the Americas.

Like the other great cultures of Central and South America, the Maya built their civilization without possessing many of the things that European and Asian peoples took for granted. They had no carts or wagons, and no large animals trained to pull a burden. Only foot travelers used their fine roads. The Maya had large, seagoing canoes for trading along their Caribbean coastline, but they never thought to capture the wind with sails. They used very little metal. Except for a few ornaments of gold and copper, stone and wood were their everyday materials.

The Maya had a more complex written language than any of the other native peoples of North and South America. Their language was based upon hieroglyphic signs, like that of the ancient Egyptians, and not upon an alphabet like the English language. Scholars today are still trying to decipher what the Maya wrote.

With their simple materials, tools, and technology, the Maya nonetheless reached a remarkable level of civilization. They built great cities with broad plazas, handsome palaces, and step-sided pyramids dedicated to their gods. Their paintings and sculptures were vivid and

*Like the Minoans, Aztecs, and ancient Egyptians,
the Maya wrote in hieroglyphics (above) instead of
using an alphabet.*

colorful. Most remarkable of all were their achievements in mathematics, astronomy, and the development of a calendar. By careful observation of the sun, moon, and stars—they had no telescopes, of course—the Mayan astronomers were able to divide the year into 365 days and could predict eclipses of the sun and moon with amazing accuracy.

Mayan civilization had its beginnings around the year 1500 B.C. and reached its most advanced state in the years A.D. 300 to 900. During this period, the Mayan population peaked at nearly 14 million and the Maya built their great cities, which sometimes were home to as many as 50,000 people each. Chichén Itzá was one of these busy cities. It is located in the north central part of Mexico's Yucatán Peninsula, the stubby arm of land that juts northward between the Gulf of Mexico and the Caribbean Sea.

Chichén Itzá was most likely founded about 1,500 years ago, and achieved its period of greatest wealth and importance about the years A.D. 1000 to 1200. Chichén Itzá was a special place for the Maya because of a single natural feature. It was the site of one of the largest of the Yucatán's odd, circular, straight-sided wells that dot the region's limestone rock as if punched out by a biscuit cutter. Chichén Itzá's *cenote* (the name the Spanish gave to the well) is roughly 180 feet across. There is a drop of about 60 feet from the lip of the well to the surface of the water and 60 feet of water below. The water came from rainfall, and from underground springs.

The cenotes of the Yucatán provided the Maya with drinking water, but that is not what made Chichén Itzá and its cenote so famous. The Mayan people believed this particular well was the dwelling place of Chac, their rain god. During times of drought, the Maya believed they had to give sacrifices to Chac to save the cornfields they depended on for food. And the great, deep well was where they offered those sacrifices.

In order to please Chac, the Maya threw golden jewelry and figurines, carvings of jade, pottery, plates of gold, and wooden idols into the cenote. But sometimes they believed that Chac demanded more. On those occasions, the Maya would toss a young man or woman, or perhaps a child, from the edge of the cenote into the murky water below. Usually the victim would struggle and drown, never to be seen again. If, however, the victim managed to remain alive upon the surface of the water, the Maya would haul the person out of the cenote and honor him or her as a messenger from Chac.

The Mayan civilization fell into decline during the 1400s, although the sacrifices at Chichén Itzá continued for another 100 years. By the time the Spanish strengthened their hold on the lands of the Maya in the 1500s, they had abandoned the old ceremonial city. But the story of the well of sacrifice survived.

Diego de Landa, the sixteenth-century Spanish bishop of the conquered territory, destroyed many of the Mayan writings. In his report to the king of Spain, he told about the offerings to the cenote and its god. "If this country possessed gold," Landa wrote, "it would be this well that would have the greater part of it." The conquerors were eager to gather as much gold as they possibly could from the lands they had claimed for Spain. But they had no way of getting to the bottom of the cenote of Chichén Itzá, no matter how much gold it might contain.

Throughout the centuries that followed, explorers were no better equipped than the Spanish to probe the cenote's gloomy depths. An American named John Lloyd Stephens visited the ruins of Chichén Itzá in 1842, but he could only wonder what lay at the bottom of the dark pool. In 1882, a Frenchman named Désiré Charnay tried to use a crude dredge (a device used for collecting debris from the bottom of a body of water) in the cenote, but he came up with nothing. And so the stage was set for the arrival of Edward H. Thompson, the first man to concentrate seriously on getting to the bottom of the sacred well of the Maya.

Edward Thompson was born in Worcester, Massachusetts in 1840. During his early twenties, Thompson wrote an article expressing his belief in the lost continent of Atlantis. The article caught the eye of Stephen Salisbury, who was affiliated with the American

Antiquarian Society in Worcester. If Thompson was interested in ancient lands, Salisbury suggested, why not do some exploring in a fascinating place that was known for sure to exist? Salisbury used his influence to have the young Thompson appointed consul (a representative of the U.S. government) in the Yucatán city of Mérida. Thompson left for Mexico when he was 25, and he spent much of the next 40 years exploring the jungle-hidden ruins of Mayan cities.

Thompson first turned his attention to Chichén Itzá in 1904. Like many amateur archaeologists in those days, including Heinrich Schliemann and Arthur Evans, Thompson solved the problem of permission to work by simply buying the place he was interested in. As the

Stephen Salisbury (1835-1905), a member of the American Antiquarian Society, encouraged Edward Thompson to become an archaeologist.

owner of the cenote, his first thought was to explore the bottom by using windmills to pump out the water, but he soon realized that this method would be too expensive. Next, he decided to use a dredge that was far more modern and effective than the one tried earlier by Charnay.

Hoisting his dredge bucket at first over the rim of the cenote, and later—because it was quicker—to a boat floating on the surface of the water, Thompson hauled load after load of muck and debris up from the bottom. Progress was slow, as the winch that raised and lowered the dredge had to be hand operated. Local Indian workers, descendants of the Maya who had once ruled Chichén Itzá, did this time-consuming work. During the first few days, as the dredge brought him nothing but mud and decayed vegetation, Thompson became discouraged. He began to worry, as he later wrote, that the traditions of the sacrifices "are simply old tales, tales without any foundation in fact."

Finally, the buckets of mud began to yield pieces of broken pottery, but Thompson was still not pleased. "Boys are boys," he observed, "whether in Yucatán or Massachusetts." Had he merely found evidence that some long-ago Mayan children had enjoyed skipping flat pieces of broken dishes across the surface of the cenote?

But Thompson's efforts were eventually rewarded. One day, while looking down at the muck brought up by the dredge, he saw a few yellowish balls made of a waxy

Edward Thompson (left) and an assistant explore the jungles that surround the ruins of the Mayan civilization in the Yucatán Peninsula.

material. He put a piece of the material into a fire, and by the sweet smell that rose into the air, he recognized the substance as a type of incense made from tree sap—a sacred incense that, according to the old legends, had been among the ritual offerings thrown into the cenote.

As the years went by, Thompson and his work crews hauled ever more fascinating objects from the bottom of the well. There were bells crafted of copper and bronze, knives made of the black volcanic glass called *obsidian*, carvings of turquoise and jade, and ornaments of pure gold. And there were human bones—bones of the unlucky Maya chosen as sacrifices to the rain god.

Thompson worked at the dredge for three years. Then, in 1907, he grew impatient with waiting at the surface for artifacts to come up in buckets of ooze and tried something far more dangerous. After taking diving lessons himself, Thompson hired a professional diver from Greece. The two men put on the clumsy diving gear of the day—canvas suits with heavy metal helmets and air hoses connected to pumps on shore. (Modern scuba equipment was developed years later.)

Thompson and his assistant became the first people to plunge into the forbidding waters since the last of the human sacrifices! The two men returned safely, but with little to show for the adventure. The cenote's water was so murky that it was all they could do to keep from getting tangled in the limbs of sunken trees, and they came back to the surface with only a few small artifacts.

Four giant staircases climb the sides of Castillo, the 79-foot building located at the center of Chichén Itzá.

Thompson's years of dredging and his brief experiment at diving yielded a wonderful collection of sacrificial objects. But he ran into a problem: By sending his finds to the United States, where many of them were exhibited at Harvard University's Peabody Museum, he angered Mexican officials who had passed a new law that made shipping historic artifacts out of the country illegal. Although Mexico could not get back what had already been sent to the United States, the Mexican government seized his property at Chichén Itzá. Several years after Thompson's death in 1935, the Peabody Museum returned many of the artifacts to Mexico. But the questions concerning the rightful ownership of archaeological treasures continued to make headlines in the years that followed.

During the late 1960s, another team of archaeologists set its sights on the sacrificial cenote at Chichén Itzá. This time, the researchers were able to use modern pumps to try to drain the well. But the underground streams that feed it replaced the water almost as quickly as they could pump it out.

Since pumping could not empty the cenote, the next plan was to treat the water with huge amounts of chlorine, a chemical used to keep the water in swimming pools clean. The chlorine would kill all life in the well, including the algae and bacteria that made the water so murky. When the waters were finally purified, scuba divers could see well enough to retrieve artifacts from the bottom.

To honor their rain god, Chac, the Maya at Chichén Itzá threw gold, jewelry, and sometimes even people into their sacred well (lower left).

Although the Spanish described this structure (photographed here by Edward Thompson) and others like it as "temples," modern archaeologists are not positive how the Maya used many of their buildings.

The plan worked, and the team added a great many metal, ceramic, and stone artifacts to what had already been collected by Edward Thompson. These archaeologists discovered that very few of the well's contents were made out of pure gold, which the Maya had possessed only in very small quantities. And, sadly, the divers' yield included a great many bones belonging to the youthful victims of Chac's deadly rituals. No matter how clear its waters could be made, the history of the sacred cenote of Chichén Itzá has remained dark indeed.

During his archaeological career, Hiram Bingham (1875-1956) took more than 17,000 photographs of his discoveries.

6

Hiram Bingham
The Inca Hideaway at Machu Picchu

*O*ne of the greatest of all archaeological discoveries was made by a man who wasn't even a trained archaeologist and who didn't have to dig so much as a shovelful of earth to make his find. The man was Hiram Bingham, and the place he found on the remote Peruvian mountaintop of Machu Picchu was the fabled hideaway of the Inca Empire.

The Incas (their name comes from the title of their ruler, the Inca) were among the most advanced of the native peoples "discovered" by the Spanish conquerors of what later became known as Latin America. The Incas had the largest pre–Columbian empire in the Americas. During the 200 years before Spanish conquerors arrived in 1532, the Incas had spread their power over much of western South America. They ruled in golden splendor from their capital of Cuzco, located in the high Andes Mountains of what is now Peru.

The Incas were great builders, farmers, and organizers. No one was ever as expert at building with large blocks of stone as the Incas were. They cut their huge stones so exactly that they did not need cement to hold them together. To this day, many buildings constructed by the Spanish after their conquest of Peru stand on solid, ancient Inca foundations.

As farmers, the Incas grew many of the food crops that people across the globe depend on today. They ate corn, peppers, peanuts, squash, and many varieties of potato. Although potatoes were unknown in Europe before the Spanish found them growing in the Incas' well-tended fields, potatoes are now a staple in the diets of many European countries.

The Incas looked upon their emperors as demigods (half humans, half gods). The emperors ruled over their vast territory with the help of a wonderful system of roads—10,000 miles in all—that crossed mountains, deserts, and jungles. Hundreds of bridges—which often resemble the hanging, swaying footpaths frequently pictured in adventure films—connected these roads across dangerous river gorges. Along these roads and bridges, messengers and soldiers could travel swiftly from Cuzco to all the provinces in the empire, while news and taxes poured back into the capital with equal speed. The Incas had nearly all the inventions that were common to sixteenth-century Europe, with three main exceptions: They did not have sailing ships, the wheel, or a written language. They moved their goods from place to place on the backs of llamas.

In the spring of 1532, the Spanish adventurer Francisco Pizarro came into the Inca Empire. Partly because the Incas had been weakened by a five-year civil war that had just ended and partly because of his own luck and daring, Pizarro and a small force of soldiers were able to conquer the empire swiftly. They captured the Inca leader himself and put him to death.

In time, the gold-hungry Spanish created their own empire out of the Inca lands. A few years after the Spanish victory, a new Inca leader took his followers deep into the mountains northwest of Cuzco. There, in a fortress-town called Vilcabamba, the rebel Incas held out against the Spanish for 30 years. But once Spain defeated the rebels in 1572, the Incas abandoned Vilcabamba, and it was lost to history among the mountains that had protected it. Eventually, the fortress became little more than a legend, something for explorers and archaeologists to dream of finding. Few people would have suspected that

Spanish conquistador Francisco Pizarro (1470?-1541), who pretended to befriend the Incas before conquering their empire, was killed at dinner one evening by a group of assassins.

Hiram Bingham III would be the one to uncover that legend.

There was little to suggest a career in archaeology in the background of Hiram Bingham III. Born in 1875 in Honolulu, Hawaii, he was the son and grandson of U.S. missionaries. The first two Hiram Binghams had been strict New England churchmen who had spent their lives bringing Christianity to the Hawaiians and other Pacific islanders. His parents had planned the same sort of life for young Hiram, who began his schooling in Hawaii and then was sent to preparatory school in Massachusetts and to Yale University.

When Hiram graduated from Yale in 1898, he returned to Hawaii to work at a Honolulu church and to prepare for further religious study. Soon, however, he changed his mind about becoming a missionary. He fell in love with a wealthy young woman from Connecticut who was visiting Hawaii with her family. Her name was Alfreda Mitchell, and Hiram Bingham had already met her briefly when he was a student at Yale. Although Hiram loved Alfreda, he knew that her father would not approve of the marriage unless he had a career that would pay more than missionary work. At first Hiram tried the Hawaiian sugar business, but he soon decided to go back to school and become a college professor. In the winter of 1899-1900, while at the University of California, Hiram chose the history of South America as the subject he would study and teach.

At the beginning of the twentieth century, U.S. colleges still had very little interest in the history of South America. In fact, when Hiram Bingham was working on his doctorate degree in history at Harvard, the university's massive library had so few books on the subject of South America that the administration put him in charge of building the collection.

As a young scholar of South American history, Bingham concerned himself primarily with what had happened on the vast continent *after* the Spanish conquerors had arrived in the early 1500s. At first, he had no interest in the native civilizations that had thrived there over the long centuries before the arrival of the Spanish. The most powerful of these peoples were the Incas. All through his student days in California and at Harvard, Hiram Bingham did not suspect that the Incas would hold the key to his future fame and glory.

Hiram Bingham married Alfreda Mitchell in 1900 and received his Ph.D. from Harvard University in 1905. That year, Princeton University's new president, Woodrow Wilson, hired Bingham to lecture at the university. (Wilson was a man with an even greater future ahead of him. In just seven years, he would be elected president of the United States.) But Bingham would not

After serving as president of Princeton University from 1902 to 1910, Woodrow Wilson was elected governor of New Jersey in 1910 and president of the United States in 1912.

spend his life in classrooms and libraries. Within two years, he would be off on his first exploration.

Bingham planned his first South American trip to learn more about the military routes followed by Simón Bolívar, the early nineteenth-century leader who fought against Spain for the independence of Colombia, Venezuela, Ecuador, Bolivia, and Peru. After following Bolívar's mountain and jungle paths and visiting the sites of his battles, Bingham hoped to write a book about the great liberator. He never wrote the Bolívar book, but he did learn that he loved an explorer's life of danger and adventure. He returned to South America as soon as he could, which was in 1909. This time, he traveled—sometimes by riding on a mule—along the old Spanish trade route from Buenos Aires to Peru. It was there, among the ruins near the old Inca capital of Cuzco, that the young American scholar became fascinated by the great, vanished empire.

Hiram Bingham returned to his home and to his growing family (he and Alfreda eventually had seven sons) and wrote a book, *Across South America*. He was already eager to revisit the high Andes, with their raging rivers, rickety rope bridges, and steep, dizzying trails. He knew in his heart that ruins even more wonderful than those he had already seen were lost among those mountains and that among them might be Vilcabamba, the last stronghold of the doomed Incas.

After studying the life of South American liberator Simón Bolívar (above), Hiram Bingham decided he wanted to become an explorer.

Bingham didn't have to wait long. Early in 1911, a group of wealthy Yale University graduates was excited by a speech he gave and offered to pay for a seven-man expedition to explore the highland domains of the Incas that summer. Hiram Bingham would lead the Yale Peruvian Expedition. This would turn out to be the high point of his life and also one of the high points of twentieth century archaeological exploration.

Bingham and his expedition partners began their work in the mountain city of Cuzco in the early summer of 1911. He immediately began questioning virtually everyone he met to see if anyone knew of any Inca ruins in the region north of the city. He was especially interested in the remote valley through which the wild Urubamba River flowed. According to missionary reports collected in the sixteenth century, an Inca city was hidden in the Urubamba valley. Professors at the university in Cuzco told him there were no ruins up that way. But one prospector who had actually visited that remote country—the professors had not—said the valley did indeed hide remains of great Inca buildings. One place the American might look, the prospector added, was a mountain called Machu Picchu.

The expedition team soon left Cuzco and made its way down the Urubamba. The roads were little more than dangerous trails hacked into the steep sides of the valley. Here and there were the scattered ruins of Inca walls and buildings, but there was nothing that could be called a city. Finally, on July 23, the tired party set up camp near a run-down inn kept by a local farmer named Melchor Arteaga, who spoke the local Indian language. Using their interpreter, the Americans told Arteaga what they were searching for. He nodded toward a mountain across the river and told the interpreter that he would lead them to ruins near its peak the next morning.

The morning of July 24, 1911, was gray and drizzly in the Andes. Along with Arteaga and a Peruvian army sergeant named Carrasco, Hiram Bingham began the climb to the heights of Machu Picchu. The journey began with a log bridge so slippery that Bingham crawled across it on his hands and knees, all the while watching the Urubamba crashing and churning through the rapids below. Then came an hour and a half of climbing on a narrow, crumbling trail that switched back and forth across the nearly vertical face of the mountain. The group reached a clearing where two farmers lived with their families. After a simple lunch of spring water and the farmers' boiled sweet potatoes, one of the farm boys came to lead Bingham and Carrasco along the final steps of the way.

And what steps they were! "We rounded a knoll," Bingham later wrote, "and suddenly faced tier upon tier of Inca terraces rising like giant stairs." These terraces, hundreds of feet long, were the level places that the Incas had carved out of the mountainside to grow their crops. On terraces like these, the Indians had grown potatoes like the ones Bingham had eaten for lunch. But the explorer could see that the terraces he now climbed had been made for growing far more than a peasant's crop of potatoes. "Enough food could be grown here," he wrote, "to feed a city."

That city lay just ahead, along a saddlelike ridge between the peaks of Machu Picchu and Huayna Picchu.

According to Hiram Bingham's account of the day, he had the following experience:

> [I was] plunged into damp undergrowth, then stopped, heart thumping. A mossy wall loomed before me, half hidden in trees. Huge stone blocks seemed glued together, but without mortar. . . . Beyond it stood another, and beyond that more again. . . . Some steps led to a plaza where white granite temples stood against the sky. . . . Down the slope, buildings crowded together in a bewildering array of terraced levels linked by at least 100 stairways.

Among the houses and terraces, streets and stairways, Bingham found what he believed must have been the palace of the Inca himself, along with a splendid stone building that he called the "Temple of the Sun." Centuries of lush plant growth partly hid these fine structures, but to Bingham they seemed not like ruins, but like buildings that had simply been abandoned by whoever had last used them. All of them were made of that wonderful Inca stonework, with blocks cut and fit together with laser-like precision. As he scrambled about taking pictures and writing in his notebook, Bingham began to wonder about the significance of Machu Picchu and wrote that it "might prove to be the largest and most important ruin discovered in South America since the Spaniards arrived."

Hiram Bingham made two more trips to Machu Picchu within the next few years—one in 1912 to clear the

The Inca city at Machu Picchu, which overlooks the Urubamba River 2000 feet below, was one of the few urban centers of pre-Columbian South America.

brush away from the buildings and another in 1915 to find the old Inca roads that had led to the mountaintop city. During these visits and in the years between, Bingham had become convinced that Machu Picchu was indeed Vilcabamba, the last stronghold of the Incas. The Spanish had never found it, he felt, and the city had simply dwindled to a ghost town after the Spanish had defeated the last Inca soldiers in the valley below. He even came up with a bolder theory that Machu Picchu was not only the place where the Incas had lived out their last days as a free people, but that it was the place where their culture had begun, hundreds of years before.

Today, experts do not think that the great realm of the Incas was born on this mountaintop. In fact, most scholars do not even think that Machu Picchu was Vilcabamba. Instead, they believe that the last stronghold was probably a ruined lowland fortress that Bingham had found a few weeks later during the 1911 trip. Experts now believe that Machu Picchu was built late in Inca history for some purpose not presently known. But experts still consider it to be the largest and most important ruin discovered in South America, just as Bingham had said it was.

Hiram Bingham went on to a long and varied career. In addition to being a professor and an author, he became a pioneer aviator who trained combat pilots during World War I, and a U.S. senator from Connecticut.

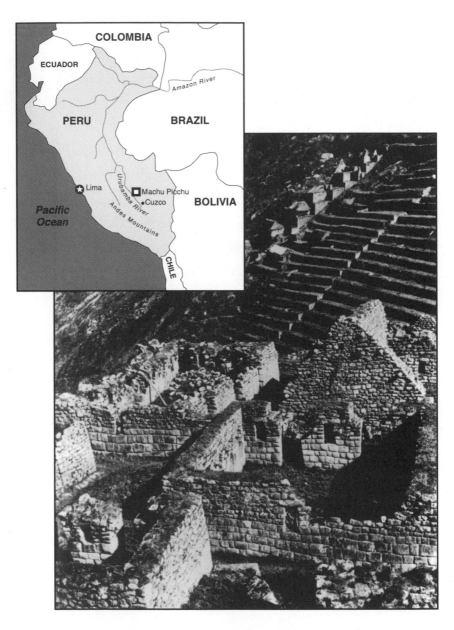

The advanced architectural design of the Inca city at Machu Picchu, which has more than 3,000 steps linking the city's many levels, impresses both archaeologists and modern architects.

But no achievement of Bingham's long life—he died in 1956—ever matched that July day in 1911.

When travelers visit Peru to see Machu Picchu today, they find a road that leads from the train station to the ruins, which are kept clear of the vegetation that concealed them for so many years. The steep road, which was opened in 1948 with Machu Picchu's aging discoverer as the guest of honor, was called Carretera Hiram Bingham.

After years of excavation in Egypt, Howard Carter (1874-1939) discovered one of history's most famous archaeological sites.

7

Howard Carter
The Tomb of Tutankhamen

*H*e wasn't a very important king, and he lived only into his late teens. Tutankhamen (also spelled Tutankhamon and Tutankhamun) was the pharaoh of Egypt for only nine years, from 1361 to 1352 B.C. Yet because of the discovery of his wonderfully preserved tomb by an English archaeologist named Howard Carter, "King Tut" has come to represent much of the mystery and glory of the ancient kingdom along the Nile River.

The Egyptians were a very religious people, and one of the main concerns of their religion was the life of

King Tutankhamen, who ruled Egypt from 1361 B.C. until his death in 1352 B.C. (when he was about 18 years old), was buried in a coffin made of gold.

the soul after death. The ancient Egyptians believed that part of their spirit remained in their bodies after they died. Thus, they thought it necessary to preserve the bodies of those who had died. This is why the process of *mummification* came into use. The more important a person was in life, the more care the Egyptian embalmers took to preserve his dead body as a mummy. No one had a higher place in the Egyptian world than the *pharaohs*, or kings. Their subjects believed the kings were gods who lived on earth, so when a pharaoh died, the Egyptians gave his mummy the most careful burial possible. Laid to rest in a specially built tomb, the mummy was surrounded with all the fine possessions the pharaoh had enjoyed in life. These things—works of art as well as useful objects—were intended to serve him in the spirit world.

Many of the tombs of ancient Egypt's pharaohs were dug into the rock walls of a place now called the Valley of the Kings. Unlike the pyramids, these tombs were not buildings. Instead, they were hidden chambers with their entrances sealed over. The Valley of the Kings lay near the west bank of the Nile River, opposite the city of Luxor, about 300 miles south of Egypt's present-day capital of Cairo. (The Egyptian pyramids, which are the tombs of the pharaohs who lived more than 1,000 years before Tutankhamen, stand much closer to Cairo.)

Throughout the Eighteenth to the Twentieth Dynasties, nearly 30 pharaohs ordered that their tombs be set into the valley walls. The lonely, barren valley seemed like a good place for the pharaohs to spend eternity with their fine possessions because if a tomb was easy to find, it would be visited by robbers. No matter how carefully the tombs of the earlier pharaohs had been sealed and guarded, sooner or later their treasures had been looted.

With the passing of time, robbers stripped even the well-hidden tombs in the Valley of the Kings of their gold, jewels, and other valuable items. By the mid-1700s, most of them had been empty for well over 2,000 years, and European travelers had already explored 14 of them. During the 1800s, the first serious archaeologists had come to the hot, dusty valley and had begun collecting artifacts from the tombs that had survived the centuries of busy robbers. By the early years of the twentieth century, many experts believed there were no more tombs left to be discovered in the Valley of the Kings, and that all of their riches were either in museums or lost to the tomb-robbers of long ago.

Into this not very promising situation came Howard Carter. Carter was born in 1874 at his parents' summer home in the county of Norfolk in England. His father, Samuel Carter, was an artist who painted animals, especially race horses that belonged to members of the nobility. When young Howard began to show a talent for drawing, his father gave him lessons. The boy never had any special education in archaeology and, unlike most children, he was taught at home by a tutor.

Howard Carter might well have followed in his father's footsteps and become an artist. But during the spring of 1891, Lady Gladys Amherst of Hackney, the wife of a nobleman named Lord Tysson Amherst, noticed the 17-year-old's work. Lord Amherst was one of the sponsors of a series of Egyptian archaeological digs. Lady Amherst asked Howard if he would like to work at the British Museum in London, helping to copy rough sketches made at the excavation sites into carefully finished drawings.

Lady Gladys Amherst of Hackney was so impressed by young Howard Carter's work that she offered him a job as an archaeological artist for the British Museum in London.

Howard Carter spent three months in London at his new job. The men Carter worked for were so pleased with his drawings that they invited him to come with them to Egypt, where he could make sketches right on the spot. Howard agreed, and in October 1891 he sailed for the land of the pharaohs.

Right from the start, Carter learned that along with his drawing chores, he would actually be allowed to join in the digging. He was fortunate to be working with a team led by one of the era's great archaeologists, William Matthew Flinders Petrie. Petrie taught his young assistant the value of patience and hard work and began showing him what to look for during the slow, painstaking progress of a dig.

With Petrie, Howard Carter helped to uncover the remains of the city of Akhetaten, which had briefly been the capital of the ancient Egyptian kingdom at the time of Pharaoh Akhenaton and Queen Nefertiti's reign during the fourteenth century B.C. While working at Akhetaten, the teenage archaeologist was shown a ring bearing the name of the little-known pharaoh Tutankhamen. Even the experts were not sure exactly when this pharaoh sat on the Egyptian throne. They did not know that he was the boy-king who married the daughter of Akhenaton and Nefertiti. And they certainly could not suspect that his long-hidden tomb would one day be found by Petrie's eager young assistant.

William Matthew Flinders Petrie (1853-1942), one of the world's leading Egyptologists during the nineteenth century, introduced Howard Carter to the field of archaeology.

Nearly all of Carter's education in the rich and complex lore of old Egypt took place under the hot desert sun at archaeological digs—not in comfortable university classrooms back home in England. After serving under Petrie, he worked for six years with another great Egyptologist, Edouard Naville. By the time he was 25, Carter had learned so much and had made such a good impression on the older men (mostly British and French) who controlled the archaeological work in Egypt, that

113

he received an important position. Carter was now the inspector of antiquities to "Upper Egypt" and Nubia. ("Upper" Egypt is actually the southern part of the country, which is farther "up" the north-flowing Nile River. Nubia is the old name for the country now called Sudan, which is even farther south.)

In 1902, Carter met with a wealthy American named Theodore Davis, who had come to Egypt a few years earlier to seek adventure as a supporter of archaeological work. In those days, rich men would select archaeology as a hobby and then would ask the government of Egypt or another country for permission to open a dig at a particular place. It didn't matter that these men were not experts themselves. They hired trained archaeologists to organize their projects and paid people to do the hard work of setting up camp, carrying supplies, and turning the desert earth with shovels. In return, the wealthy men would have their names attached to any big discoveries their people might make. And perhaps they might also take home priceless artifacts for their private collections. (At that time, an excavation's sponsor was allowed to keep half of what was found.)

Carter was able to retain his job with the Egyptian government's department of antiquities while working for Theodore Davis as director of a new dig. The site of the dig was in the Valley of the Kings, where few people thought there was much left to be found.

Working with Davis, Howard Carter uncovered the valley tombs of Pharaoh Tuthmosis IV and Queen Hatshepsut. Both of these tombs had long before been robbed of their burial treasures, but their discovery at least proved that the Valley of the Kings might still be guarding some secrets. The excavation of Hatshepsut's tomb was a special triumph for Carter, because it lay at the end of a passageway 200 yards long and nearly 100 yards deep. The passage was filled with so much rock and soil that the project took part of two winter digging seasons. (No one was able to work during the brutal heat of the Egyptian summer.)

Despite his successes with Davis's excavations, the years following the Hatshepsut discovery in 1904 were not good ones for Howard Carter. First, the government transferred him to a new post in northern Egypt, a place that did not interest him nearly as much as the Valley of the Kings. Then, in 1905, he lost his job because he had done it too well. When he had ordered guards to send away a group of disorderly French tourists who had tried to push their way into a site without buying tickets, a fight broke out and the tourists complained to their government. Carter refused to apologize for the incident and resigned from his position instead.

Carter spent the next few months earning his living by selling paintings to tourists who came to Luxor. Then, another wealthy patron came into his life. His name was George Edward Stanhope Molyneux Herbert, the Fifth Earl of Carnarvon.

The Earl of Carnarvon had been working at Egyptian archaeological digs each winter since 1903. His great love was collecting, and rather than stay at home and wait for finds to be presented to him, he spent a great deal of time at his desert sites—though not, of course, with a shovel in his hands. In 1906, he was seeking both permission to dig in the Valley of the Kings and also a trained archaeologist to take charge of his project. When he asked the director of the department of antiquities whom he might recommend, he was given the name of Howard Carter. Lord Carnarvon followed the suggestion; Howard Carter and Lord Carnarvon would work together for the next 14 years.

The first seven of those years saw no great discoveries. Under Carter's direction, Carnarvon's workers had uncovered and opened tomb after tomb, only to find that robbers had been ahead of them by centuries. At several sites, the men uncovered inscriptions that helped to explain ancient Egyptian history, but Lord Carnarvon was only interested in objects, not in inscriptions. By 1914, he was ready to give up on the Valley of the Kings. But Howard Carter still held out hope that a great find could be made there. He and Carnarvon were about to give it one more try when the First World War temporarily put an end to archaeological work.

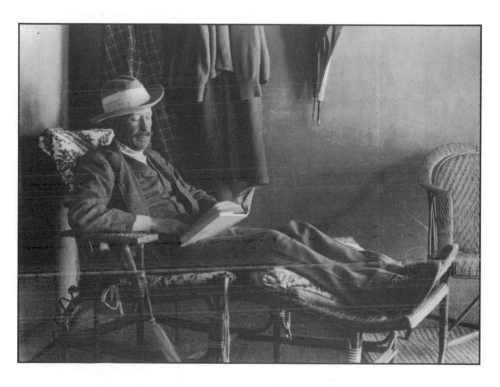

Lord Carnarvon relaxes at Howard Carter's home in Egypt.

By the end of the war in 1918, Howard Carter still had hopes for one site in the Valley of the Kings. "I had always had a kind of superstitious feeling," he later wrote, "that in that particular corner of the valley one of the missing kings, possibly Tutankhamen, might be found." The place that most interested him was near the already explored tomb of Pharaoh Ramses VI. There, he had discovered the foundation ruins of workers' huts, probably used by the builders of Ramses's tomb. Could they possibly be concealing an earlier, still undiscovered tomb? In 1922, he convinced Lord Carnarvon to try one last dig in the Valley of the Kings.

With Lord Carnarvon still in England, Carter and his crew began digging near Ramses's tomb in November 1922. Their luck took hold right away. Beneath the first of the hut foundations, they came upon a flight of steps leading down to a sealed doorway. In all of his years in Egypt, Carter had never found a royal tomb with its seal unbroken. He immediately chiseled a small hole in the wall near the top of the doorway. Thrusting in a flashlight, he looked and saw that the passageway on the other side was filled with small stones and broken rock. This was a good sign since tomb builders had usually blocked entranceways in just such a manner to make it harder for thieves to break in.

Carter would have loved to continue digging, but he was sure Lord Carnarvon would want to be at his side. He sent him a telegram, and Carnarvon arrived in Luxor by November 23. The next day, the two men were at the mysterious staircase, watching as workmen uncovered more of the door. More seals came into view, and several of them had the name Tutankhamen written on them.

Two days later, Carter's crew broke through the door at the bottom of the stairs and began moving away the rubble in the passageway beyond. By this point, Carter and Carnarvon had begun to notice evidence that robbers had gotten into the tomb after all. Several holes had been plastered over, and some of the door seals were actually resealings. But as the work progressed, it became clear that the robbery had taken place a very long time ago, perhaps only a few years after Tutankhamen's death. The robbers had upset some of the articles in the tomb's outer chambers, but they had not gotten away with much. Royal officials had resealed the tomb, and it had been lost to history—and to robbers—when rubble from the building of Ramses's tomb had covered its entrance.

Now Carter and Lord Carnarvon could see an inner door, and it too bore the seals of Tutankhamen. Carter chipped a hole in an upper corner of the door and poked into the space beyond with an iron rod. Nothing blocked the way. The archaeologist carefully chiseled away until the hole was large enough for him to peer through. Holding a candle, Carter was quiet for a moment. All was silent until Lord Carnarvon asked, "Can you see anything?"

"Yes," answered Carter. "Wonderful things."

*These lids, which were designed to resemble
Tutankhamen and buried in his tomb, covered jars
containing the pharaoh's internal organs.*

They were wonderful things indeed. Tutankhamen
had been sent off to the afterlife with chairs and couches
ornamented with carved animals' heads, chests and vases
made of the marblelike stone called *alabaster,* and life-
sized statues with gold-leaf robes and sandals. The
pharaoh's royal throne was inlaid with gold. Most exciting of all, there was a second sealed door on the opposite
side of the room. The robbers from long ago had broken
a hole through the wall next to it, but the room beyond
was still filled with treasures they were not able to take.

Howard Carter opens the door to one of the inner shrines within the tomb of Tutankhamen.

Among these were statues of the pharaoh, beautifully painted wooden boxes, splendid chariots, and a throne of wood worked with gold, glass, and precious stones. But off to the right in the first room, there was yet another sealed door.

One of the objects found in Tutankhamen's tomb was a statue of Sekhmet, a lion-headed goddess in Egyptian mythology who could both cause and cure widespread disease.

This third door, Carter believed, led to the actual burial room. But there was so much work to be done in carefully photographing and removing the articles from the two outer rooms that it was February 1923—three months later—before they could open the final door. (Archaeological work is slow, and things have to be done in the proper order to avoid mistakes and confusion.) During the winter months of 1922 and 1923, Howard Carter must have been glad he had learned to be patient and meticulous during 30 years in Egypt.

Carter's patience was rewarded when he opened the final door. Within this third room stood what looked like a wall of solid gold, which turned out to be part of a gold-covered shrine built to cover the *sarcophagus*, the stone box surrounding Tutankhamen's coffin. But the golden panels were only the outermost walls of the shrine. By the time Carter had carefully worked through to the sarcophagus itself, during the following winter, he had opened the bolts and seals of four separate shrines, each set within the other like nesting puzzleboxes.

When workers lifted the great granite lid of the sarcophagus, the situation was much the same. Within were three separate coffins, one inside the other. The first was covered with sheet gold, made into a beautiful likeness of the young king. On the image's forehead was a wreath of flowers, perhaps placed there by Tutankhamen's wife. The second coffin was very similar and lay nested closely within the first. But it was surprisingly heavy! Inside,

Howard Carter and one of his assistants examine the coffin of Tutankhamen.

Carter knew, there could be room for only one more coffin and the mummy itself. He soon realized that the coffin had weighed so much because the innermost coffin was made of solid gold.

Inside the third coffin, a mask of solid gold, inset with colored glass and semiprecious stones, covered the mummy's head and shoulders. The mummy itself would later be unwrapped in a laboratory. There Howard Carter would first see the face of the king who had died 3,300 years earlier—yet who had strangely influenced the direction of so much of Carter's own life and work.

It would be several more years before all of the archaeological work at the burial site would be completed. The treasures of Tutankhamen's tomb would be examined and removed for preservation. Until his death in 1939, Howard Carter would spend much of his time thinking and writing about the great discovery.

Lord Carnarvon never saw the gold coffin. In April of 1923, less than half a year after the discovery of the tomb, he died in Cairo of a fever. Because he had gotten sick so quickly and died so soon afterward, there was much talk of his being the victim of a "pharaoh's curse." There were, indeed, many old Egyptian warnings about disturbing the tombs of kings. And, in fact, a number of archaeologists working in Egypt did die young. Howard Carter himself lived for 16 years after discovering Tutankhamen's tomb, and he died at the age of 64.

Tourists visit the Valley of the Kings, which served as the burial site for Egypt's pharaohs beginning around the year 2500 B.C.

Some scientists have suggested that perhaps some unfamiliar and deadly germ was locked away in the dead, still air of the tombs. Others think that the ancient Egyptians might have put poison on some of the surfaces in the hidden rooms. Or maybe Lord Carnarvon merely died of an infected mosquito bite, as doctors suspected at the time. Other archaeologists were the victims of accidents and diseases that had nothing to do with old superstitions. The final answer is still a mystery— hidden, as Tutankhamen's tomb was, in the Valley of the Kings.

Kathleen Kenyon (1906-1978), who discovered the oldest known town in human history at Jericho during the 1950s, continued to receive international attention after making significant archaeological finds in Jerusalem during the 1960s.

8

Kathleen Kenyon
The Biblical City of Jericho

"Jericho," wrote the British archaeologist Kathleen Kenyon, "can make the proud claim to be the oldest known town in the world."

Kathleen Kenyon, who was one of the world's greatest experts on the history of that city, spent much of the 1950s excavating the older "Jerichos" that lay buried near the present-day city. She even found evidence that people have been living at this spot for more than 11,000 years. Jericho lies 15 miles northeast of Jerusalem on the floor of the great, deep valley through which the Jordan River flows on its way from the Sea of Galilee to the Dead Sea. The Dead Sea—so called because its waters are too salty to support life—is the lowest place on the earth's surface, almost 1,300 feet below sea level. Jericho itself is 800 feet below sea level, which makes it not only the oldest town in the world, but also the lowest.

The plain where Jericho is located is almost a desert, with dry white soil, fierce temperatures, and barely eight inches of annual rainfall. Of all the places on earth—all of the green valleys and the cool, breezy hillsides—this seems the least likely place to hold the title of "oldest town." But for centuries the Wadi Qelt spring, which is fed by a natural underground reservoir, has made Jericho an oasis in the desert. For this reason, the region must have attracted settlers not long after human beings first learned to plant crops and keep their animals in one place.

It isn't necessary, however, to go back to the earliest days of Jericho's settlement to understand the special historical interest it holds. Jericho is one of the places most frequently mentioned in the Old Testament of the Bible. The most famous reference, of course, has to do with the walls of Jericho falling before the attacking Israelites, as Joshua and his men blew their battle horns.

Archaeologists have often felt a strong attraction to explore biblical sites—an attraction that goes beyond the religious interest of Jews, Christians, and, to some extent, Muslims. (The Muslims' sacred book, the *Koran*, recognizes many of the events described in the Bible.)

According to the Bible, the walls of Jericho fell when Joshua, leader of the Israelites, led an attack on the Canaanite city.

For whatever one may believe about the Bible's religious messages, its text is also a key to the history of the peoples and places of the Middle East. A place like Jericho, with a history rooted in early biblical times and extending through the eras of the Romans and medieval crusaders right into today's newspaper headlines, is sure to be a fascinating place for an archaeologist to dig.

Archaeologists have been doing just that for more than 100 years. They already knew that the site of the Jericho mentioned in the Bible is at a slightly different location than the modern city of the same name. Religious pilgrims to the region had noticed that fact as early as the fourth century A.D. Those travelers long ago observed that the ruins of old Jericho were hardly visible and therefore must lie buried beneath the ground.

In 1868, the English captain Charles Warren conducted the first scientific dig at an earthen mound called Tell es-Sultan, located outside the present-day city of Jericho. Warren first dug trenches in an east-west direction across the mound and then in a series of eight-foot-wide shafts. He found pottery jars and tools for grinding corn, but not much else. He also struck part of a stone wall, whose age he couldn't identify. But archaeology was not very precise then. Had Warren's understanding been more advanced, he might have known that some of the pottery he found dated to the New Stone Age (8000 to 6000 B.C.), long before biblical times. The wall was more recent, however. Kathleen Kenyon would later identify it as having been built during Palestine's early Bronze Age, which lasted roughly from 3100 to 2300 B.C.

Further excavations were made throughout the late nineteenth and early twentieth centuries. As so often happens in archaeology, the more we learn, the more complicated everything becomes. By 1950, archaeologists knew there were not merely two Jericho sites— ancient and modern—but a jumble of them, close to and even overlapping each other. Scholars argued about both the dates of various unearthed ruins and the year that Joshua and the Israelites attacked the old city occupied by the Canaanites, a people who may have been related to the ancient Assyrians of Mesopotamia. Jericho, which had looked above ground to be no more than a quiet village, turned out to be a complicated place indeed once workers turned over a few shovelfuls of earth.

Kathleen Kenyon began her excavations at Jericho in 1952 and worked there until 1956. The British School of Archaeology in Jerusalem organized her expedition, which involved the help of many other institutions and individuals. Kenyon's expedition also had the support and participation of the kingdom of Jordan, which at that time held the territory in which Jericho was located. Archaeology had changed vastly since the days when a wealthy amateur could simply buy a site, hire a few local laborers, and begin digging on his own. Archaeologists no longer could excavate sites and take artifacts as they pleased, with little regard for local authority.

During her four years of work, Kenyon and her team learned as much about Jericho as had been discovered over the previous century of study. In some places, the workers dug all the way to bedrock, 50 feet below the surface. Kenyon was able to sort out the artifacts and building fragments of different periods and identify the locations of the Jerichos of different eras. She also found the earliest traces of human occupation of the site, proving its claim, as she wrote, to be the "oldest known town in the world."

Heading backwards through history, there are three basic Jericho sites, and all are within a few miles of each other. The modern town is built along the Wadi Qelt stream that flows into the Jordan River. This settlement, largely inhabited by Palestinian Arabs, is built on the site of a town established in the late Middle Ages by European crusaders, the warriors who came to seize the Holy Land (now Israel) from the Muslims.

Before the Jericho of the crusades, there stood the Jericho of Herod the Great—the same King Herod who figures in the biblical story of the birth of Jesus Christ. Herod rented the site of Jericho from Cleopatra, the queen of Egypt, and built a small Roman-style city there. This Jericho, where Herod died in 4 B.C., stood on the Wadi Qelt a mile upstream from the modern town. It was eventually destroyed by Persian and Arabian invaders.

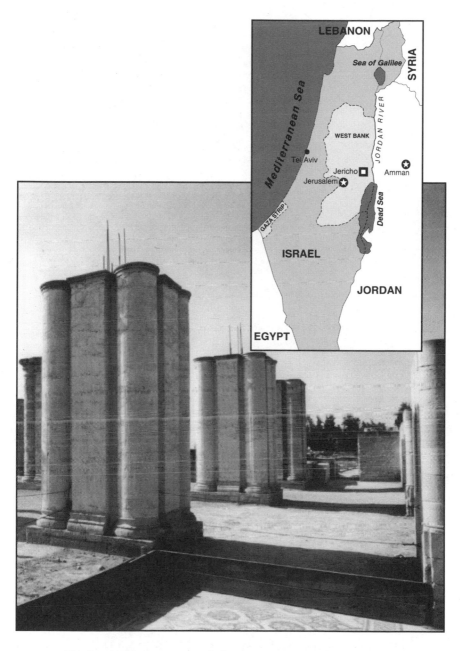

Hisham's Palace, one of the many ancient buildings at Jericho, was destroyed soon after its construction in A.D. 724, but it was restored years later.

*These ruins show the elaborate designs that decorated
the walls of Hisham's Palace at Jericho.*

A final stop on this backwards-through-time tour
of the Jerichos is that great mound of Tell es-Sultan,
where Kathleen Kenyon and earlier archaeologists had
dug their trenches and shafts. The mound stands nearly
two miles northeast of Herod's Jericho. Apart from a
few scattered houses and some graves dating to the
Roman Era, some 2,000 years ago, Kenyon found little
evidence that the mound site was occupied later than
about 600 B.C., when King Nebuchadnezzar of Babylon
deported the Hebrews of Judah to Babylon. This
"Babylonian captivity" lasted until 57 B.C.

The city that had stood there before had been built
about 880 B.C. Erosion has carried away most of the

remains of this Iron Age settlement, which according to the Bible was built by a man from Bethel named Hiel. For roughly 500 years before Hiel restored Jericho, nothing had been built upon the ruins of the walled city of the Canaanites that Joshua had destroyed. According to the Bible, Joshua had placed a curse on anyone who should build up Jericho again, and Hiel lost two sons because of the curse.

But when did Joshua fight the battle of Jericho? Kathleen Kenyon's best estimate is that the walls fell— very possibly by earthquake— a few years before 1300 B.C. But the ruins of the walls are gone, perhaps lost to the

During his reign from 605 B.C. until his death in 562 B.C., King Nebuchadnezzar of Babylon was the most powerful ruler of western Asia.

erosion of centuries. In her book *Digging Up Jericho*, though, Kenyon tells of finding the ruins of a house at this level of excavation, with a small broken pottery jug lying on the floor. Kenyon suggests that the ruin might be "part of the kitchen of a Canaanite woman, who may have dropped the juglet beside the oven and fled at the sound of the trumpets of Joshua's men."

Kenyon dug deeper, delving into the Jericho of the Middle and Early Bronze Age (which began in approximately 3500 B.C.). Much of the story of the city's life in the Bronze Age, prior to the conquest by Joshua and the Israelites, was told in the contents of the tombs of that era. The wealthier inhabitants of Jericho buried their dead with bowls and jars made of white alabaster, wooden combs, wooden boxes inlaid with bone, woven clothing, and furniture made of the wood of various trees.

The Middle Bronze Age was a time of fine pottery-making in Palestine. Archaeologists have found numerous graceful and delicate bowls, jugs, and vases within these tombs. Like well-trained archaeologists working in other parts of the world, Kenyon used the various ceramic objects she found to help her estimate the dates of the tombs and the buried ruins she found.

In the later part of the Middle Bronze Age, about 1700 B.C., Jericho was a thriving, prosperous town. Kenyon's dig uncovered evidence of the town's growth during this period and of the strengthening and expansion of its walls. Throughout the Bronze Age, beginning around 3100 B.C., Jericho grew from a town into a city. As the city expanded, its walls became more important, both as a defense against rival towns and as protection against nomadic raiders.

Sometimes the walls protected the citizens of Jericho, and sometimes they did not. Kenyon's careful inspection of the ruins showed that fire destroyed the walls during certain periods. How can a fire destroy walls of mud bricks? The builders had strengthened the brick walls with heavy wooden timbers, which caught fire when attackers set their torches to bundles of brush set outside the walls. Sometimes even the houses built close to the inside of the wall would ignite. To a trained eye like Kenyon's, the reddened bricks and the brush fire ashes told how fiercely the fire had blazed.

Deeper excavations at Jericho turned up fragments of the city's life in far earlier times. Kenyon learned that she could divide the New Stone Age (approximately 8000 to 6000 B.C.) in Jericho into a later period (when the inhabitants used pottery) and into an earlier time (before people learned this craft). The oldest building at Jericho has been dated to 9250 B.C. Sifting through the remains of this earliest Jericho was like looking through a window at a distant time when a few family groups first stopped wandering from oasis to oasis and settled near the reliable spring to irrigate their gardens and grow a steady supply of food. As others joined them, a town came into being.

Archaeologists uncover a circular tower (lower left) that stood at Jericho around 7500 B.C., almost 2,000 years after humans had settled the first town at that site.

Working close to bedrock, Kenyon and her team found what was left of the houses of that town. They had been made of hand-shaped, sun-dried clay bricks, set on foundations of stone. Their plaster-floored rooms were arranged around a central courtyard, where the people of that first Jericho lit fires to cook their meals. Even the ashes remain. Around these fires, as dusk settled over the Jordan valley, the town of Jericho was born.

Major Archaeological Finds
Across the Globe

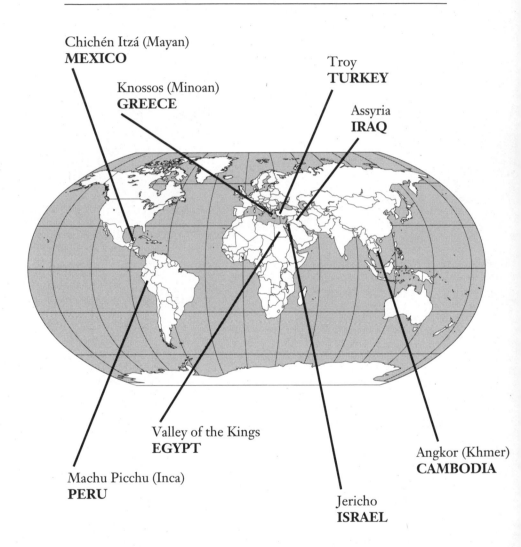

Chichén Itzá (Mayan)
MEXICO

Knossos (Minoan)
GREECE

Troy
TURKEY

Assyria
IRAQ

Valley of the Kings
EGYPT

Angkor (Khmer)
CAMBODIA

Machu Picchu (Inca)
PERU

Jericho
ISRAEL

Since the mid-nineteenth century, archaeologists have made major finds across the globe, continually adding to our knowledge of the past.

142

Time Line of Ancient Civilizations

Most dates are approximations. Entries in **bold face** are described in this book.

c. 1.7 million B.C.
First signs of *australopithecus* and *homo habilis*—early hunters and gatherers.

c. 70,000 B.C.
Early humans, called *homo erectus*, begin using fire and advanced tools.

c. 35,000 B.C.
Earliest signs of modern humans, called *homo sapiens*, in Africa and southern Europe and Asia.

c. 30,000 B.C.
Humans travel across the Bering Strait during the first wave of migration from northeast Asia to North America.

c. 10,000 B.C.
Humans establish semi-permanent settlements in ancient Mesopotamia (the present-day Middle East).

c. 9250 B.C.
Jericho, perhaps the first permanent community in human history, thrives near the Dead Sea in present-day Israel.

c. 8000 B.C.
Numerous tribes of people occupy North and South America.

c. 6000 B.C.
Humans begin settling on the island of Crete off the coast of Greece.

c. 3700 B.C.
Mesopotamians invent the wheel.

c. 3500 B.C.
Permanent agricultural settlements are established in Egypt.

c. 3000 B.C.
The people of Mesopotamia write the *Epic of Gilgamesh*.

c. 2500 B.C.
Pharaohs begin ruling Egypt and, following their deaths, are preserved as mummies.

c. 2350 B.C.
Egyptians begin inscribing hieroglyphics on the walls of their pharaohs' tombs to protect them in the afterlife.

c. 2300 B.C.
Fire sweeps through the thriving city of Troy, leaving many inhabitants no time to take their valuables with them.

c. 2000 B.C.

The Minoan people build elaborate palaces on the island of Crete, including the palace at Knossos.

c. 1800 B.C.

The Assyrians rise to power in Mesopotamia.

c. 1375 B.C.

The palace of Knossos is destroyed—perhaps by an earthquake or volcanic eruption.

1361 B.C.

King Tutankhamen dies after serving as Egypt's pharaoh for nine years.

c. 1300 B.C.

As told in the Old Testament of the Bible, Joshua destroys the walled city of Jericho, and the site remains unoccupied for 500 years.

c. 1190 B.C.

According to legend, invaders from Greece destroy the city of Troy, an event later known as the Trojan War.

c. 1000 B.C.

Hebrew elders begin writing the Old Testament of the Bible.

c. 750 B.C.

Greek poet Homer writes the *Iliad*, an epic poem about the siege of Troy.

616 B.C.

Nearby enemies invade and destroy the Assyrian Empire, located in present-day Iraq.

c. 400 B.C.

In the *Timaeus* and the *Critias*, Greek philosopher Plato writes about the imaginary civilization of Atlantis that sank beneath the sea, a story that may have been inspired by the Minoans on the island of Crete.

c. 300 B.C.

Invention of the Mayan calender, which is much more precise than any previous calendars.

1 A.D.

The first year of the "common era"—all dates that follow are A.D. rather than B.C.

79

Mount Vesuvius erupts, burying the Roman city of Pompeii in a deep layer of ash.

c. 350

Chichén Itzá, the center of Mayan civilization, flourishes on the Yucatán Peninsula in Central America.

900

Yasovarman rules Angkor (in present-day Cambodia) and founds its first capital city.

c. 960

Mayan culture declines, and the Maya abandon the city of Chichén Itzá.

c. 1150

The largest Hindu temple in Asia is constructed in the Khmer capital of Angkor Wat.

1177

King Jayavarman VII establishes the new capital city of Angkor Thom.

c. 1200

The Inca Empire develops in the area of present-day Peru.

c. 1440

Angkor is abandoned after an attack by invaders from Siam (now Thailand).

The Inca Empire expands in South America.

1492

Christopher Columbus sets sail for the West Indies, but reaches the Americas instead—probably the first contact between Europeans and Native Americans.

c. 1500

Archaeology begins developing into a field of study after Italian scholars take an interest in ancient Greek culture.

1532

After the arrival of Spanish explorer Ferdinand Pizarro, Spanish conquerors massacre the Incas, whose empire stretched more than 2,000 miles in South America.

1692

When an earthquake strikes the Jamaican capital of Port Royal, the city sinks in the waters of its harbor.

1845

Austen Henry Layard discovers the palaces of Assyrian kings Sargon and Ashurnasirpal II.

1860

French naturalist Henri Mouhot discovers the remains of the city of Angkor.

1871

Heinrich Schliemann begins excavating the ruins of Troy.

1872

Scholars translate the *Epic of Gilgamesh*, written on the tablets found by archaeologist Hormuzd Rassam.

1900

Arthur Evans begins digging on the island of Crete and eventually uncovers the palace of Knossos.

1909

Edward Thompson and his assistants find golden jewelry and human bones at the bottom of the sacred Mayan well at Chichén Itzá.

1911

Hiram Bingham discovers the fortress city of the ancient Incas at Machu Picchu.

1922

While digging in the Valley of the Kings, Howard Carter finds the tomb of Tutankhamen.

1952

Kathleen Kenyon and her team of archaeologists begin excavating ancient Jericho, which Kenyon describes as "the oldest known town in the world."

Bibliography

Audric, John. *Angkor and the Khmer Empire*. London: Robert Hale, 1972.

Bartlett, John R. *Jericho*. Grand Rapids: William B. Eerdmans, 1982.

Bingham, Alfred M. *Portrait of an Explorer: Hiram Bingham, Discoverer of Machu Picchu*. Ames: Iowa State University Press, 1989.

Brackman, Arnold C. *The Dream of Troy*. New York: Mason and Lipscomb, 1974.

Ceram, C.W. *Gods, Graves, and Scholars: The Story of Archaeology*. New York: Knopf, 1951.

Clancy, Flora S., et al. *Maya: Treasures of an Ancient Civilization*. New York: Abrams, 1985.

Coggins, Clemency Chase, and Orrin C. Shane III. *Cenote of Sacrifice: Maya Treasures from the Sacred Well at Chichen Itza*. Austin: University of Texas Press, 1984.

Cohen, Daniel. *Hiram Bingham and the Dream of Gold*. New York: M. Evans, 1984.

Evans, Joan. *Time and Chance: The Story of Arthur Evans and His Forebears*. London: Longmans, Green and Co., 1943.

Freeman, Michael, and Roger Warner. *Angkor: The Hidden Glories*. Boston: Houghton Mifflin, 1990.

151

Horwitz, Sylvia A. *The Find of a Lifetime: Sir Arthur Evans and the Discovery of Knossos*. New York: Viking, 1981.

Kenyon, Kathleen M. *Digging Up Jericho: The Results of the Jericho Excavations, 1952-1956*. New York, Praeger, 1957.

Michailidou, Anna. *Knossos: A Complete Guide to the Palace of Minos*. Athens: Ekdotike Athenon S.A., 1985.

Payne, Robert. *The Gold of Troy: The Story of Heinrich Schliemann and the Buried Cities of Ancient Greece*. New York: Funk and Wagnalls, 1959.

Reeves, Nicholas. *Treasures of Tutankhamun*. New York: Metropolitan Museum of Art, 1976.

Schliemann, Heinrich. *Ilion, the City and Country of the Trojans*. New York: Arno, 1967.

Thompson, Edward Herbert. *People of the Serpent: Life and Adventure Among the Mayas*. Boston: Houghton Mifflin, 1932.

Vandenberg, Philipp. *The Golden Pharaoh*. New York: Macmillan, 1980.

Waterfield, Gordon. *Layard of Nineveh*. New York: Praeger, 1968.

Willard, Theodore Arthur. *The Sacred Well*. New York: Century, 1926.

Index

excavation of, 23-26, 28
Noah, 19, 28, 29
Nubia, 114

obsidian, 84
Odyssey, 51
Old Testament, 15, 130,
    See also Bible
Oxford University, 64

paleontology, 9
Palestine, 133
Paris, of the *Iliad*, 52-53
Peabody Museum, Harvard
    University, 86
Peru, 91, 92, 97, 105
Persia, 19, 20
Petrie, William Matthew
    Flinders, 112, 113
pharaohs, Egyptian, 64,
    107, 108, 109-110, 112,
    See also Tutankhamen
"pharaoh's curse," 125
Phnom Penh, 42
Pizarro, Francisco, 93, 94
Plato, 72-73
Pompeii, 11
Port Royal, 11
potatoes, 92, 100
pottery, 8, 9, 58, 66, 68, 79,
    82, 132, 138
Priam, 52, 54; palace of,
    54; treasure of, 54, 58
Princeton University, 96
pyramids, Egyptian, 9, 109

Ramses VI, 118, 119
Rassam, Hormuzd, 16, 26,

27; and story of
    Gilgamesh, 26, 28, 31
robbers, 110, 116, 119, 120
Roman Era, 53, 64, 132
Russia, 50

St. Petersburg, 50
Salisbury, Stephen, 80-81
sarcophagus, 123
Sargon II, 16, 20
Schliemann, Heinrich, 46,
    65, 81; belief of, in
    Homer's stories, 48, 51,
    52, 56, 58; as
    businessman, 50, 56;
    death of, 59; early years
    of, 46, 48-49; education
    of, 48, 51; excavations of,
    at Hissarlik, 52, 53-54,
    56, 58; search for Troy,
    52-54, 56
sculpture, 21; at Angkor,
    37, 43; Assyrian, 21, 22,
    23, 24, 25
Sekhmet, 122
Sennacherib, 16, 24; palace
    of, 24-26
Siam, 33-34, 42
Sir Stratford, *See* Canning,
    Stratford
Smith, George, 28
Sorbonne, 51
South America, 76, 92, 95,
    97, 98, 102
Spanish conquest, 75, 79-
    80, 92, 93, 95, 96, 103
Sparta, 53
Stephens, John Lloyd, 80

157

Photo Credits

Photographs courtesy of Griffith Institute, England: pp. 6, 117; Mickey Jones Photography, pp. 8, 10, 12 (both), 108, 120, 122, 126; National Portrait Gallery, England, pp. 14, 18, 27, 74, 111; Hood Museum of Art, Dartmouth College, Hanover, NH, Gift of Sir Henry Rawlinson through Austin H. Wright, Class of 1830, pp. 22, 25; The Bettmann Archive, pp. 29, 30, 46, 49, 55, 59, 94, 98, 102, 131, 137; Topham Picture Source, England, p. 32; Roger-Viollet Documentation Photographique, France, pp. 36, 38, 41, 44; Ancient Art and Architecture Collection, England, pp. 57, 73; Ashmolean Museum, England, pp. 60, 67 (both), 68, 69, 71; Dover Pictorial Archive Series, pp. 62, 77; Embassy of Mexico, Washington, DC, p. 85; American Antiquarian Society, pp. 81, 83; Peabody Museum, Harvard University, pp. 87, 88; National Geographic Society and Peabody Museum, Yale University, p. 90; Library of Congress, p. 96; University Museum, University of Pennsylvania, pp. 104, 113; Metropolitan Museum of Art, pp. 106, 121, 124; Institute of Archaeology, University College London, p. 128; Israel Government Tourist Office, pp. 135, 136, 140.

ABOUT THE AUTHOR

WILLIAM G. SCHELLER, an experienced science and travel writer, is the author of numerous magazine articles and more than 20 books, including *The World's Greatest Explorers*. Scheller is also co-author of *Columbus and the Age of Discovery*, a companion volume to the highly acclaimed public-television series of the same name. He visited North American archaeological sites while working on that book. Scheller lives in northern Vermont with his wife and son.